Rapid Vocabulary Builder

NORMAN LEWIS

A PERIGEE BOOK

To Carolyn Russell

Perigee Books
are published by
The Putnam Publishing Group
200 Madison Avenue
New York, NY 10016

Library of Congress Cataloging-in-Publication Data

Lewis, Norman, date.
  Rapid vocabulary builder.

  Reprint. Originally published: New York: Grosset &
Dunlap, 1975.
  "A Perigee book."
  Includes index.
  1. Vocabulary.   I. Title.
PE1449.L45   1988   428.1   87-10817
ISBN 0-399-51400-7

Printed in the United States of America
      4   5   6   7   8   9   10

Contents

Books by Norman Lewis

Rapid Vocabulary Builder, revised edition
Word Power Made Easy, revised edition
The New Roget's Thesaurus in Dictionary Form, revised edition
How to Read Better and Faster, fourth edition
R.S.V.P. for College English Power, Books I, II, III
Instant Spelling Power for College Students
See, Say, and Write! Books I, II
R.S.V.P.—Reading, Spelling, Vocabulary, Pronunciation, Books I, II, III
Thirty Days to a More Powerful Vocabulary (with Wilfred Funk), revised edition
The Modern Thesaurus of Synonyms
The New Power with Words
Thirty Days to Better English
How to Become a Better Reader
New Guide to Word Power
Dictionary of Modern Pronunciation
Correct Spelling Made Easy
Dictionary of Correct Spelling
Better English
Twenty Days to Better Spelling
How to Get More Out of Your Reading
How to Speak Better English
The Lewis English Refresher and Vocabulary Builder
Power with Words
Journeys Through Wordland, Books I, II, III, IV
Vocabulary and Spelling, Books I, II

How to Use This Rapid Vocabulary Builder

This book has been designed for quick and successful learning. It discusses 130 basic forms plus 160 or more derived forms, for a total of close to 300 useful, valuable, exciting words—the kind of words that belong in the functional vocabulary of the person who wishes to express his or her thoughts effectively.

These words are divided into twenty-four separate units, and each unit can be studied and successfully mastered in an average time of twelve to fifteen minutes. This is the kind of book that can be picked up at odd moments during the day, that can turn short stretches of spare time into enriching learning experiences.

It has been my aim throughout these pages to explain each word so completely and so clearly that it will become a permanent part of the reader's thinking, speaking, reading, and writing vocabulary. A word is discussed in detail, with particular emphasis on its application to actual use and on its relevance to real-life situations. The emotional background of the word is explored wherever possible, and its special connotations thoroughly investigated. Next comes a general definition, followed by easily understood pronunciations of all its forms, plus a brief note on the source from which the word entered the English language. Whenever necessary, spelling, usage, or pronunciation cautions are appended so that students will feel fully confident that they can put the word or any of its forms into immediate and correct use, whether spoken or written.

At the end of the discussion of each group of five to ten words, the readers are invited to check on their learning by taking the series of tests that round out each Unit. In the True and False quizzes, they react to the meaning of the word in typical sentence patterns; meet its synonyms and antonyms in a Same and Opposite quiz; next have a chance to use the word directly by completing meaningful sentences; and finally test their recall and understanding of the word when offered a brief definition.

Periodically throughout the book are comprehensive review tests (six in all, one at the end of each Part) which offer further checks on learning, and at the end there is a final examination which covers every word discussed in all twenty-four units.

The techniques used in this book are those I have found most effective with the thousands of students I have taught, over the past 30 years, at the City College of New York, New York University, and Rio Hondo College in Whittier, California. The reader will not, I hope, consider me presumptuous if I express a belief that these techniques are particularly successful in any intensive vocabulary-building program.

Without conscious effort, the average adult adds twenty-five to fifty new words to his or her vocabulary in a year's time; this book is so set up as to offer the reader a chance to learn, in a very short time, as many new words as he or she might normally acquire in several years.

PRONUNCIATION SYSTEM

I. VOWEL SOUNDS

SYMBOL	EXAMPLE
A, a	hat (HAT)
E, e	met (MET)
I, i	sit (SIT)
O, o	not (NOT)
U, u	nut (NUT)
AH, ah	far (FAHR)
AI, ai	fair (FAIR)
AW, aw	fort (FAWRT)
AY, ay	fate (FAYT)
EE, ee	feet (FEET)
	richly (RICH'-lee)
$\bar{\text{I}}$, $\bar{\text{i}}$	sigh (S$\bar{\text{I}}$)
	prize (PR$\bar{\text{I}}$Z)
ING, ing	making (MAYK'-ing)
$\bar{\text{O}}$, $\bar{\text{o}}$	smoke (SM$\bar{\text{O}}$K)
$\overline{\text{OO}}$, $\overline{\text{oo}}$	moon (M$\overline{\text{OO}}$N)
O͝O, o͝o	look (L$\breve{\text{OO}}$K)
OW, ow	spout (SPOWT)
OY, oy	noise (NOYZ)

II. CONSONANT SOUNDS

SYMBOL	EXAMPLE
B, b	beet (BEET)
D, d	deaf (DEF)
F, f	far (FAHR)
G, g	give (GIV)
H, h	high (HI)
J, j	just (JUST)
K, k	quickly, cave (KWIK′-lee, KAYV)
L, l	love (LUV)
M, m	march (MAHRCH)
N, n	not (NOT)
P, p	pen (PEN)
R, r	rough (RUF)
S, s	sighs (SĪZ)
T, t	try (TRĪ)
V, v	view (VYOO)
W, w	wary (WAIR′-ee)
Y, y	yellow (YEL′-o)
Z, z	zenith (ZEE′-nith)
SH, sh	contentious (kən-TEN′-shəs)
	licentious (lī-SEN′-shəs)
TH, th	thing (THING)
	atheist (AY′-thee-ist)

III. THE SCHWA(ə)

The symbol ə, called a *schwa*, indicates a very brief vowel sound in an unaccented syllable.

acerb	ə-SURB′
adultery	ə-DUL-tə-ree
bigamy	BIG′-ə-mee

IV. ACCENT

The accented syllable of a word is printed in capital letters and is followed by the accent mark:

admonish	əd-MON′-ish
celibate	SEL′-ə-bat

In a word with *two* accented syllables, capital letters plus the accent mark (') indicate the stronger accent; lower case letters plus the accent mark (') indicate the weaker accent.

choreographer   kaw'-ree-OG'-rə-fər
incongruity   in'-kə-GROO'-ə-tee

ABBREVIATIONS

n. for *noun*
v. for *verb*
adj. for *adjective*
adv. for *adverb*
pl. for *plural*

PART I

People

CONSIDER THE FOLLOWING:
A *celibate* existence
Lives *frugally* on his pension
Decorous behavior
A *docile* child
Iconoclastic and rebellious adolescent
Diffident and self-effacing manner
Full of *vindictiveness*
An *acerb* remark
The *phlegmatic* northern races
Unable to cope with his *recalcitrant* pupils
An unusually *verbose* answer
Sanctimonious pretense
Inane and irrelevant statement
Dour parents
A *dogmatic* statement
Has always lived *indolently*
Intransigent opposition
Felt most *contrite*
A *puerile* sense of humor
That *contentious* bore!

Do you know what these phrases REALLY mean?
Could you use them correctly and EFFECTIVELY?

Read on . . .

Unit One

1. CELIBATE

As everyone knows, there are two sexes. In the natural order of things, a member of one sex eventually develops certain more or less intimate emotional ties with some member of the opposite sex. Such ties, if legally consummated, are encouraged by society and by the culture in which we live.

It is considered that many advantages accrue to the wedded state. Statistics show that married people live healthier lives (other things being equal), are less likely to commit suicide, occupy fewer beds in our mental hospitals, and are in general better adjusted to the outside world.

Also, they often have children, thus providing work and income for doctors and dentists, clothing manufacturers, nursery-furniture stores, and milk companies.

There are, of course, obvious disadvantages to the wedded state— but we needn't go into those here.

A small minority of adults, for one reason or another, figure that the disadvantages outweigh the advantages. These adults lead a *celibate* existence—they do not marry. Moreover, they do not engage in love affairs, and they have as little to do with the opposite sex as the circumstances of their lives make possible. Consciously, their *celibacy* is voluntary; how much they are at the mercy of their unconscious in not seeking out a mate is another question.

Celibacy can also be involuntary.

In a prison, for example, *celibacy* is enforced. For another example, men and women in the armed forces generally lead a *celibate* existence, on a perhaps less than voluntary basis.

Members of various religious orders must take vows of *celibacy;* and, occasionally, spinsters or bachelors may be *celibates* because no one feels inclined to accept them as romantic or marriage partners.

Though the primary meaning of *celibate* is unmarried, you cannot with any logic refer to a single man or woman as *celibate* simply because he (or she) has made no legal commitments; only that adult who assiduously avoids, or is denied, all romantic encounters with the opposite sex may be called *celibate*.

DEFINITION

Celibate means: unmarried; vowed to remain single; totally lacking in romantic attachment to any member of the opposite sex.

PRONUNCIATIONS

Celibate	SEL′-ə-bət
Celibacy	SEL′-ə-bə-see

PRONUNCIATION CAUTIONS

When a noun ends in *-ate*, such as *graduate*, *estimate*, *associate*, the final syllable is correctly pronounced in a close approximation of the word *it*.

THUS:

A college *graduate*—GRAJ-ŏŏ-ət
A rough *estimate*—ES′-tə-mət
His new *associate*—a-SŌ′-shee-ət

However, the verb form of such words ends in the sound *ayt*.

THUS:

To *graduate* with honors—GRAJ′-ŏŏ-ayt′
To *estimate* roughly—ES′-tə-məyt′
To *associate* with doctors—ə-SŌ′-shee-ayt′

The following are important *exceptions*. These nouns have the *ayt* pronunciation:

A *candidate* for re-election—KAN′-də-dayt′
An Indian *potentate*—PŌ-tən-tayt′
An *inmate* of the institution—IN′-mayt′
A well-known *magistrate*—MAJ′-əs-trayt′

DERIVATION

Latin *caelebs*, unmarried.

2. FRUGAL

You have doubtless known people who, because of circumstances beyond their control, are forced to husband their resources with great care.

They never waste food or money, nor do they prematurely discard any possessions which still have some use left in them.

They're no tightwads; they're not misers. It's just that, because of a dollar shortage, they prefer to face reality and to restrict their spending to the unavoidable essentials; and they want to get the most out of what they've bought so they won't too soon have to buy more.

They spend wisely and cautiously and only when there is no alternative—for their cash is limited and they have to stretch it as far as possible, or maybe (with an ingenuity that would amaze you) a little farther.

They do not believe in feast today and famine tomorrow.

To express it all in one word, they lead a *frugal* life.

They eat *frugally,* set a *frugal* table; the food will be nourishing, but plain and inexpensive, and calculated as to quantity.

In general, they will avoid all lavishness and unnecessary expenditures.

To speak of someone's *frugality* is to show a certain admiration for his ability to make do with the little money he has.

DEFINITION

Frugal means: exercising economy; practicing great thrift; sparing in the use of something.

PRONUNCIATIONS

Frugal	FROO′-gəl
Frugally	FROO′-gə-lee
Frugality	froo-GAL′-ə-tee

DERIVATION

Latin *frugalis,* temperate.

3. DECOROUS

Most of us do not get roaring drunk every Saturday night. We do not give riotous wild parties that keep the neighborhood awake till dawn.

We do not make overt and noisy advances to our neighbor's wife, steal his car or lawn-mower, nor commit mayhem* upon his children.

*See Unit 24.

We are civil and courteous to strangers, and lose our tempers within the bosom of our families no more frequently than is fitting and proper.

And our language is comparatively free of obscenity and blasphemy.

In short, we do not act in such a way as will cause our pictures to appear in the tabloids or our names in the gossip columns.

This ideal state of affairs may have come about because most of us are essentially peaceful and decent; or possibly because we have learned that it is wise and profitable to observe those rules of behavior which the community considers dignified.

To sum it up in a single word, we live *decorously*.

Or we lead a life of *decorum*.

Or our actions are *decorous* at all times.

Or, finally, we are never guilty of *indecorous* behavior.

DEFINITION

Decorous means: proper; becoming; suitable; with dignity and propriety.

PRONUNCIATIONS

Decorous	DECK-er-us or de-KORE-us
Decorum	de-KORE-um
Decorously	DECK-er-us-lee or de-KORE-us-lee

DERIVATION

Latin *decor*, comeliness, suitability.

4. DOCILE

"Do what you're told!" is a frequently heard command in many homes where there are growing children.

If enough unreasonable strictness and domination are exercised with a youngster, he may react in one of two ways.

He may become rebellious, resistant to all authority, stubborn, and domineering in his turn when the chance occurs.

Or, on the contrary, he may become unusually pliant, obedient, manageable, and excessively subservient. (Such an attitude, say the psychologists, is fundamentally unhealthy, and may conceal deep unconscious hostility.) He may, in short, become *docile*—his spirit has been broken.

Docile people sometimes wonder why they are not more popular—after all, they never make any trouble for anyone.

They fail to realize that most of us feel only contempt for *docility*. We find nothing admirable or necessarily likable in the person who is willing to be pushed around, who does what he is told out of fear of offending us.

The *docile* child may keep the domestic hearth peaceful—but intelligent parents will not welcome too much *docility* in their children. It's poor upbringing that doesn't allow a youngster some room for self-expression, for release of tension and hostility.

And the *docile* wife may satisfy the unconscious needs of a certain type of husband—may even satisfy her own unconscious urge to self-punishment.*

But to her friends she is usually a terrific bore.

DEFINITION

Docile means; amenable to training or handling: easily managed; obedient and nonresistive.

PRONUNCIATIONS

Docile	DOS′-əl
Docility	də-SIL′-ə-tee

PRONUNCIATION CAUTIONS

THUS:
docile—DOS′-əl
hostile—HOS′-təl
servile—SUR′-vəl
futile—FYOO′-təl

However, the final syllable of the following important *exceptions* rhymes with *mile, style*.

exile—EKK-syle
senile—SEE-nyle
profile—PRO-fyle
infantile—IN-fan-tyle
reconcile—RECK-in-syle
crocodile—KROCK-o-dyle

*See *masochism*, Unit 15.

Latin *docere*, to teach. A *docile* person is easily taught, hence easily managed.

5. ICONOCLASTIC

There are some people whose chief delight seems to derive from poking fun at the cherished beliefs of others.

They are happy only when rebelling against constituted authority or established custom—and they sneer, in no mild language; at those of us who are content to accept life as it is.

They totally disagree with, and therefore violently attack, any venerated customs or accepted traditions, holding that these are usually obstacles to progress and freedom.

Such people are *iconoclastic*.

Unlike Dale Carnegie, the *iconoclast* does not believe in making friends or influencing people.

No—*his* greatest talent is for destructiveness; and since his most frequently employed weapons are sarcasm and cynisicm,* he is, as you can imagine, far from popular and less than comfortable to have around.

The *iconoclast* mocks religion, morality, convention, marriage, family, patriotism, and any other attitudes or institutions that many of us are attached to.

Adolescents are more addicted to *iconoclasm* than their elders.

While *iconoclastic* attitudes are normal to adolescence, *iconoclasm* is considered a sign of immaturity in adulthood.

DEFINITION

Iconoclastic means: assailing traditional beliefs; habitually mocking, and refusing to conform to, convention.

PRONUNCIATIONS

Iconoclastic	ī-kon′-ə-KLAS′-tək
Iconoclast	ī-KON′-ə-klast′
Iconoclasm	ī-KON′-ə-klaz′-əm

*See Unit 13.

DERIVATION

From two Greek words: *eikon,* a religious image; and *klastes,* a breaker.
An *iconoclast* is, fundamentally, a violator of religious restrictions
and, by extension, a rebel against tradition and authority.

Test Your Learning

I TRUE OR FALSE?

1. *Celibacy* is a natural condition for most people.　　*True False*
2. If one's income is ample, one needn't practice *frugality.*　　*True False*
3. Hollywood celebrities are noted for preserving their *decorum.*　　*True False*
4. *Docility* often marks the brow-beaten child.　　*True False*
5. *Iconoclasm* is a sign of maturity.　　*True False*

II. SAME OR OPPOSITE?

1. Celibate—married　　*Same Opposite*
2. Frugal—lavish　　*Same Opposite*
3. Decorous—dignified　　*Same Opposite*
4. Docile—obedient　　*Same Opposite*
5. Iconoclastic—rebellious　　*Same Opposite*

III. USE THE WORD

1. Philip Wylie's _____ attacks on American life in his satiric book, *Generation of Vipers,* have endeared him to a certain segment of the reading public.
2. In the armed forces, many men chafe under their enforced _____.
3. People on relief must live most _____.
4. Figures in the public eye find it wise and expedient to live lives of outward _____.
5. The child was so unusually _____ that the psychiatrist suspected tremendous depths of repressed hostility.

IV. WRITE THE WORD

1. The philosophy which attacks tradition, customs, and convention　　1. _____
2. Manageable, obedient　　2. _____
3. Unmarried; uninvolved with the opposite sex　　3. _____

4. Observing the proprieties; dignified   4. _____

5. Thrifty; economical; sparing   5. _____

Check Your Learning

ANSWERS TO TESTS ON UNIT 1

TEST I

1—false, 2—true, 3—false, 4—true, 5—false.

TEST II

1—opposite, 2—opposite, 3—same, 4—same, 5—same.

TEST III

1—iconoclastic, 2—celibacy, 3—frugally, 4—decorum, 5—docile.

TEST IV

1—iconoclasm, 2—docile, 3—celibate, 4—decorous, 5—frugal.

6. DIFFIDENT

Some people approach new experiences full of self-assurance, completely confident in their ability to be successful. Others, on the contrary, are weighed down with self-doubts, with feelings of inadequacy; they are constantly beset by fears that they won't be able to measure up. They speak in low, almost inaudible tones, would rather die than address a public gathering, are silent and uncomfortable in a social group, never stop trying to explain and justify their existence.

Such people are *diffident*—they carry shyness and self-effacement to a pathetic, almost ridiculous, extreme. They express their opinions *diffidently*, accept praise or assurance (if at all) with the greatest of *diffidence*. Their entire attitude shouts at you, "I am no good!"

What has brought them to this sorry condition? Childhood experiences, say the psychoanalysts—deep, hurtful, experiences with parents who criticize and sneer. How often have you heard a mother (or father, of course) say to a child, "Oh, how stupid you are!" "Why can't I ever trust you?" "Why can't you ever do anything right?" A child thus condemned accepts unconsciously the parental verdict—and turns into the insecure, painfully shy, unhappy (in a word *diffident*) adult.

DEFINITION

Diffident means: unusually shy and timid because of feelings of inadequacy; retiring; lacking in self-assurance.

DERIVATION

Latin, *dis*, not, plus *fides*, faith. The *diffident* person has no faith in himself.

PRONUNCIATIONS

Diffident	DIF'-ə-dənt
Diffidence	DIF'-ə-dəns
Diffidently	DIF'-ə-dənt-lee

7. VINDICTIVE

"I'll get even, I'll give two for one, I'll never forgive anyone who insults, or wounds, or in any way offends me, I'll carry a grudge till I die!" These are the feelings of the *vindictive* person. Handle him gently, tactfully, carefully—for any slight, whether real or imagined, will evoke swift, violent, and petty retaliation. Someone who is *vindictive* usually feels slights where no slight is intended, finds offense where no offense was given, is insulted where no insult was offered. And because he is *vindictive*, he reacts almost instinctively with thoughts of revenge. *Vindictiveness*, of course, is not a quality that endears such a person—he has few friends and many enemies. And most people find it wise to avoid him whenever possible.

DEFINITION

Vindictive means: revengeful, spiteful, retaliatory, bearing a grudge.

DERIVATION

Latin *vindicta*, revenge, punishment.

PRONUNCIATIONS

Vindictive	vin-DICK-tiv
Vindictiveness	vin-DICK-tiv-ness
Vindictively	vin-DICK-tiv-lee

8. ACERB

People are odd.

Some are perpetually gay, charming, bubbling over with good spirits, with laughter and friendliness.

Others are sharp-tongued, sarcastic, biting; their reaction to almost anything is the caustic retort, the acid comment.

These latter can best be described as *acerb*. Their *acerbity* may result from any number of conditions—ill-health, resentment, general hostility to the world, poor digestion, a compensation for deep feelings of inferiority, etc.—but whatever the cause, the manifestation is the same: bitter, sour, snappish, stinging, harsh speech.

Acerbity may be a permanent characteristic of some personalities, or it may be purely temporary—but permanent or temporary, it is intended to inflict a wound. One reacts with *acerbity*, gives an *acerb* answer, makes an *acerb* remark, etc. Bear in mind that when you describe someone as *acerb*, you are referring exclusively to the content and manner of his *speech*.

DEFINITION

Acerb means sour, bitter, caustic, sharp-tongued.

DERIVATION

Latin, *acer*, sharp.

PRONUNCIATIONS

Acerb	ə-SURB′
Acerbity	ə-SURB-ə-tee

9. PHLEGMATIC

Have you ever known someone who, in temperament and constitution, seems so emotionally dulled that you often want to light a firecracker under him just to see him react normally? In situations to which most of us respond with whoops of joy, he is maddeningly calm, unmoved. Conversely, circumstances or conditions which touch us deeply, which make us feel anguish or despair or deep despondency, leave him completely cold and unresponsive. He simply does not, probably cannot, react emotionally to anything—good, bad, or indifferent. He is more like a vegetable than a human being, never shows anger, pity, delight, fear, hurt, love, or any other sharp emotion. He is, in a word, *phlegmatic*—and you sometimes wonder why he bothers to stay alive.

DEFINITION

Phlegmatic means: stolid, impassive, temperamentally or constitutionally unemotional.

DERIVATION

Greek *phlegma*, phlegm. Ancient philosophers believed that an excess of phlegm in the body made one dull, unable to respond emotionally. (This belief is, of course, erroneous.)

PRONUNCIATION

Phlegmatic	fleg-MAT′-ək

10. RECALCITRANT

A well-adjusted child, brought up in a household where he has all the love he needs, where he gets from his parents the sense of security and belonging so vital to childhood, generally turns into a cooperative, peaceful, self-realized adult.

On the contrary, the child who has to submit to excessive discipline and harshness, who finds the parental world cold and unyielding, becomes either excessively docile or unusually *recalcitrant*.

The *recalcitrant* child is uncooperative, unruly, stubbornly disobedient, mulish, rebellious to authority, ungovernable, hard to manage.

Recalcitrance in an adult is similar to that in a child; it implies active and violent resistance to authority or defiance of another's will. We speak of a *recalcitrant* person, or a person behaving *recalcitrantly*, only if he is in a position which demands obedience to, or cooperation with, some higher authority: as a *recalcitrant* prisoner, a *recalcitrant* servant, a *recalcitrant* worker, a teacher whose general *recalcitrance* leads her principal to ask for her discharge or transfer.

As children are commonly expected to follow the dictates of parents, household, and school, we often speak of a *recalcitrant* child, a *recalcitrant* student, etc. (Incidentally, it is amazing how *unrecalcitrant* children are when they sense that you love them and when you have captured their confidence. *Recalcitrance* is an unnatural reaction, a psychological defense against emotional difficulties.)

DEFINITION

Recalcitrant means: willful; unruly; uncooperative; stubbornly disobedient.

DERIVATION

Latin *calx*, heel. The *recalcitrant* person kicks up his heels and refuses to obey.

PRONUNCIATIONS

Recalcitrant	rə-KAL′-sə-trənt
Recalcitrance	rə-KAL′-sə-trənce
Recalcitrantly	rə-KAL′-sə-trənt-lee

Test Your Learning

I. TRUE OR FALSE?

1. *Diffident* people are usually aggressive.   True   False
2. If someone has a reputation for being *vindictive*, he is
   likely to forgive insults.   True   False
3. An *acerb* remark is conducive to good relations.   True   False
4. A *phlegmatic* person is outwardly calm and placid.   True   False
5. It is difficult to control a *recalcitrant* child.   True   False

II. SAME OR OPPOSITE?

1. Diffident—retiring   Same   Opposite
2. Vindictive—retaliatory   Same   Opposite
3. Acerb—diplomatic   Same   Opposite
4. Phlegmatic—high-strung   Same   Opposite
5. Recalcitrant—docile   Same   Opposite

III. USE THE WORD

1. The foster mother, knowing the child had been subjected to harsh discipline, was prepared for _____ and hostility.
2. He responded to our offer of friendship with sneering _____.
3. _____ ly, he expressed an opinion on the subject.
4. Don't be so _____ ; I didn't mean to offend you!
5. Nothing ever excites her; she is the most _____ person I know.

IV. WRITE THE WORD

1. Unemotional   1. _____
2. Timid, unsure   2. _____
3. Unruly, unmanageable   3. _____
4. Sharp-tongued, acid   4. _____
5. Vengeful   5. _____

Check Your Learning

ANSWERS TO TESTS ON UNIT 2

TEST I

1—false, 2—false, 3—false, 4—true, 5—true.

TEST II

1—same, 2—same, 3—opposite, 4—opposite, 5—opposite.

TEST III

1—recalcitrance, 2—acerbity, 3—diffidently, 4—vindictive, 5—phlegmatic.

TEST IV

1—Phlegmatic, 2—diffident, 3—recalcitrant, 4—acerb, 5—vindictive.

11. VERBOSE

You ask some people a question—and their response is direct, to the point, immediately understandable, and containing no more words than are necessary to make their meaning perfectly clear.

On the other hand, unfortunately, there are many speakers whose minds and emotions are so confused that they use words, whether they realize it or not, to confuse and bedevil and bore their listeners. They use far more words than are needed to explain their thoughts; they are dull, repetitious, obscure—and after they have said their say you are never quite sure what they really meant, because, probably, they're not quite sure themselves.

Such speakers (or writers) can best be characterized by the adjective *verbose*. It is likely that *verbose* people use words either as a camouflage to conceal their true meaning, or as an indication of their own mental confusion.

Verbosity is a characteristic of maladjusted people, says Wendell Johnson. In his excellent book, *People in Quandaries*, Dr. Johnson makes this interesting observation: "For practical purposes, *verbose* individuals may be classified roughly into three categories. There are those who talk mainly to avoid silence. There are others who use language chiefly to conceal truth. And, finally, there are those whose incessant talking appears to serve the function of a great nervously twitching proboscis with which they explore unceasingly in search of certainty."

Needless to say, a social evening spent with a *verbose* individual is a form of mental torture to which few sane people would knowingly submit a second time.

DEFINITION

Verbose means: wordy; using many unnecessary or meaningless words.

PRONUNCIATIONS

Verbose	vər-BŌS′
Verbosity	vər-BŌS-ə-tee

Latin *verbosus*, full of words.

12. SANCTIMONIOUS

Picture an absolute model of well-advertised virtue, of publicly flawless morality, of ostentatious holiness. And then realize that this is all a sham, a pretense, a complete hypocrisy. With that contradiction between fact and appearance in mind, you will have a clear understanding of the meaning of *sanctimony*.

The *sanctimonious* person is a fraud—his "holier than thou" attitude masks a character that is no better than average, no more moral than yours or mine, and perhaps, for all we know, not as good.

Call a man *sanctimonious*, refer to his attitudes, his objections, his answers, or his actions as *sanctimonious*, and you indicate that you are perceptive enough to have penetrated behind his mask—his piety, his holiness, his moral rectitude haven't deceived you one bit, much as they may defraud the rest of the world. Call a man *sanctimonious* and you simultaneously call him a hypocrite; you are saying that his self-publicized virtue is a veneer that you don't trust and won't be taken in by.

DEFINITION

Sanctimonious means: pretending holiness; falsely pious, virtuous, or moral.

PRONUNCIATIONS

Sanctimonious	sank′-tə-MŌ-nee-əs
Sanctimony	SANK′-tə-mo′-nee
Sanctimoniously	sank′-tə-MŌ-nee-əs-lee

DERIVATION

Latin *sanctus*, holy.

13. INANE

"How can you be so *inane*?" is a question you might ask when someone annoys you with the pointlessness, senselessness, and general stupidity of his remarks. An *inane* remark, an *inane* question, an *inane* statement is utterly devoid of common sense, shows no thinking or intellectual grasp of an issue, and is generally characteristic of what we call an empty-headed person. Such a statement may be called an *inanity,* and when you say that someone's conversation is full of *inanities* you are delivering as devastating and derogatory an insult as is possible in the English language.

Similarly, writing of any sort, a letter, a paragraph, a book, etc., can also be termed *inane.*

DEFINITION

Inane means: silly, pointless, lacking in sense or point.

PRONUNCIATIONS

Inane	in-AYN′
Inanity	in-AN′-ə-tee
Inanities	in-AN′-ə-teez

DERIVATION

Latin *inanis,* empty.

14. DOUR

The expression on his face indicates, to even the most casual observer, that he sees no pleasure, no laughter, no merriment in life.

His countenance looks harsh, stern, forbidding, uncompromising—and if appearances are not deceiving he leads a rigid, humorless, strict, and fairly friendless existence. It is never any fun to be in his company—for you will search in vain for tenderness, indulgence, or gentleness. All is severity. Indeed, his personality can aptly be compared to the bleak moors of northern Scotland, the region from which we get the word which best describes him. That word is *dour.*

DEFINITION

Dour means: strict, harsh, gloomy, severe, grim, with strong implications of sternness and obstinacy, and possibly sourness of disposition.

PRONUNCIATION

Dour   Rhymes preferably with *poor,* although the pronunciation that rhymes with *sour* is also acceptable.

Originally from Latin *durus*, hard, but more directly from Scotch.

15. DOGMATIC

It may be only one man's opinion—but it is absolutely, 100% correct.

Hence, there is no arguing, no room for qualification, no slightest possibility of error. For the opinion is voiced as if it were an indisputable, unchangeable fact.

(You know the childhood story about the youngster who asked an adult for the time. When told it was eight o'clock, the child replied, "Oh no, it can't be. I'm supposed to be home at eight o'clock, and I'm not home yet!")

The *dogmatic* person, the individual who is in the habit of making *dogmatic* statements or assertions, utters his opinions as if they were matters of recorded fact, as if they were, indeed, the revealed word of God. His attitude is excessively, obnoxiously positive and arrogant, and it is plain that he will be unsympathetic to any argument or objection— what he says must be true and completely accurate (so his manner indicates) or he wouldn't be saying it. The implication in his tone is that only a fool would think otherwise or would fail to agree with him. Most people, of course, react negatively to *dogmatism,* realizing that the *dogmatic* speaker has a closed mind and is often so unconsciously insecure about the worth of his opinions that he is unable to leave the door open for further discussion.

DEFINITION

Dogmatic means: opinionated, arrogantly assertive, expressing an opinion with such a tone of finality as to leave no room for qualification or disagreement.

PRONUNCIATIONS

Dogmatic	dog-MAT'-ək
Dogmatism	DOG'-mə-tiz-əm
Dogmatically	dog-MAT'-ək-lee

DERIVATION

Greek *dogma*, originally derived from the Greek verb *dokein*, to think.

Test Your Learning

I. TRUE OR FALSE?

1. *Verbose* people are economical in the use of words.   *True   False*
2. A *sanctimonious* person is sincerely moral and virtuous.   *True   False*
3. An *inane* remark is pointless.   *True   False*
4. Children are usually happy when brought up by *dour* parents.   *True   False*
5. *Dogmatic* statements generally stimulate lively conversation.   *True   False*

II. SAME OR OPPOSITE?

1. Verbose—wordy   *Same   Opposite*
2. Sanctimonious—hypocritical   *Same   Opposite*
3. Inane—meaningful   *Same   Opposite*
4. Dour—pleasant   *Same   Opposite*
5. Dogmatic—diffident   *Same   Opposite*

III. USE THE WORD

1. We hate to get into any kind of discussion with Saul—his _____ statements and positive air make him difficult to talk to.
2. What a (an) _____ remark! You don't sound very intelligent when you talk that way.
3. His _____ bores you to death—he repeats himself, he uses ten words where one would do, and you get tired trying to fathom his meaning.
4. His _____ attitude makes it clear that he has a patent on virtue.
5. He's a (an) _____ and silent man, rarely given to laughter, stern with his children, severe in his attitude to life and pleasure.

IV. WRITE THE WORD

1. Foolish, senseless, empty   1. _____
2. Harsh, severe, forbidding   2. _____
3. Wordy, obscure   3. _____
4. Excessively positive in expression of opinions   4. _____
5. Making a false pretense of morality, holiness, or virtue   5. _____

Check Your Learning

ANSWERS TO TESTS ON UNIT 3

TEST I

   1—false, 2—false, 3—true, 4—false, 5—false.

TEST II

1—same, 2—same, 3—opposite, 4—opposite, 5—opposite.

TEST III

1—dogmatic, 2—inane, 3—verbosity, 4—sanctimonious, 5—dour.

TEST IV

1—inane, 2—dour, 3—verbose, 4—dogmatic, 5—sanctimonious.

16. INDOLENT

What does he probably like best? Lying in a hammock under a shady tree, reading a light (but *very* light) novel. For even thinking is a chore.

What does he most want to avoid? Exertion, movement, any kind of expense of energy.

He's lazy, of course—but "lazy" is too weak a word to describe him. "Laziness" implies a disinclination to work, a preference for idleness and dawdling. *Indolence* goes further: it connotes an aversion toward any kind of effort, mental or physical, work or play, pleasant or unpleasant. The *indolent* person wants to take it easy all his life.

We have little respect for the *indolent* individual, but perhaps he's happier than the person with drive and ambition.

Or maybe he just has an underactive thyroid gland.

DEFINITION

Indolent means: lazy, listless, disinclined to effort or exertion.

PRONUNCIATIONS

Indolent	IN'-də-lənt
Indolence	IN'-də-ləns

DERIVATION

Latin *dolore*, to feel pain. The prefix *in* makes the verb negative—*indolence*, by derivation, signifies *feeling no pain*, from which the actual meaning is a natural extension.

17. INTRANSIGENT

Once he has arrived at his position, especially if it is political in nature, no one can budge him.

He simply won't compromise—not by one inch.

Is he a conservative? Then he's conservative right down the line, and no amount of persuasion or reasoning will change his attitude.

Is he a reactionary? Again, no compromise with changing circumstances, with new influences, with modern times.

Or perhaps he is a radical. He is then equally unyielding, equally stubborn, equally uncompromising.

The *intransigent*, then, is politically uncompromising. *Intransigence* is a blind, unyielding adherence to political or party principles, an unwillingness to make or accept even reasonable or sensible changes. An *intransigent* attitude is stubborn, set, uncompromising, practically pigheaded.

Though the word is generally restricted to politics, it may also be used to describe any kind of stubborn unwillingness to compromise or change.

DEFINITION

Intransigent means: stubbornly unwilling to compromise.

PRONUNCIATIONS

Intransigent	in-TRAN′-sə-jənt
Intransigence	in-TRAN′-sə-jəns

DERIVATION

Latin *transigere*, comes to an agreement, plus *in*, a negative prefix.

18. CONTRITE

In a moment of thoughtless cruelty, you have administered a harsh rebuke to your young child, whose face immediately mirrors the emotional shock and pain of someone who expected love and understanding but received, instead, a slap. As you see the tears welling in the child's eyes, the acute unhappiness registered in his facial contortions (you know how pathetic, and lovable, a youngster looks as he winds up to cry), you are stung with remorse, and you gather him into your arms to comfort and console him.

One word alone accurately describes your feelings and actions in these circumstances: *contrition*.

Do something to wound someone, commit any act of cruelty or

unkindness, be guilty of any sin or crime—and then feel remorse and compunction and, in addition, a desire to make amends; you are then *contrite* over your misdeed.

You are, in short, *contrite* over something you have done, something which you later realize was ethically, morally, or socially wrong, and for which you are prepared to take active steps of atonement. *Contrition*, then, is a sense of guilt which causes deep sorrow and a desire to repent. We may speak of a *contrite* sinner, of a look of *contrition*, or we may say that a callous person feels no *contrition* over what he has done.

Note the important distinction between *contrition* and feelings of regret or unhappiness. If you had been planning an important picnic for a particular day, and the morning started out cold and rainy, you would of course be sorry. Since, however, you were not the cause of the bad weather, you would not be *contrite*.

Or if someone you loved became ill and died, you would be deeply unhappy; but again, since you were not the cause of his death, you would not feel *contrite*.

Contrition is sorrow or unhappiness for an act which you have committed, which you now regret, and for which you wish to atone.

DEFINITION

Contrite means: affected with remorse; saddened by a sense of guilt; humbly penitent over a misdeed. Generally followed by the preposition *over*, as in "He was *contrite over* his needless cruelty to his wife."

PRONUNCIATIONS

Contrite	kən-TRĪT′
Contrition	kən-TRISH′-ən

DERIVATION

Latin *contritus*, bruised.

19. PUERILE

Here is a grown man, seemingly mature (at least physically), yet in many circumstances acting like a callow youth. If he doesn't get his own way, he frets and sulks; his behavior at times reminds you of the behavior of a boy of ten. His emotional shallowness, fondness for practical jokes, and constant interest in horseplay; his excessive selfishness, total inconsideration of others, and lack of sensitivity to the needs or feelings of his fellow man betoken a juvenility of mind which is both annoying and contemptible.

Such a man is *puerile*. Since the word comes from the Latin *puer*, boy, we usually restrict its use to the male sex, and always employ the epithet derogatively.

Now it is no sin to be boyish. To have the freshness and vigor, the optimism and ambition and unbounded confidence of youth is admirable, more often than not. But in young boys there are many unpleasant characteristics, characteristics we expect from an adolescent, but for which we feel contempt if they linger on in the adult. Such annoying characteristics, which most boys eventually grow out of, mark a man as *puerile* if he still retains them when he has reached the age of maturity. So *puerile* and *puerility* are always terms of deep contempt and generally applied to men. (Girls, for some reason or other, always seem to mature at a satisfactory rate, some of them growing up suddenly and unexpectedly, both physically and emotionally. Of course there are immature women, but they apparently keep their immaturity so artfully concealed that the English language has felt no need to find a special word for them.)

DEFINITION

Puerile means: childish, foolish, unthinking, immature, acting like a callow youth in circumstances in which adult behavior is expected. Applied to men, and always a term of contempt.

PRONUNCIATIONS

Puerile	PYOO′-ə-rəl *or* PYOOR-əl
Puerility	pyoo-ə-RIL′-ə-tee *or* pyŏŏr-IL′-ə-tee

DERIVATION

Latin *puer*, boy.

20. CONTENTIOUS

You have, no doubt, often met (and always to your sorrow) that unpleasant mortal who can turn the most innocent discussion into an argument, a violent dispute, a heated controversy. If someone has committed the blunder of inviting him to a friendly social gathering, it is not very long before he has made the evening difficult for everyone by his eternal habit of disagreeing and debating and wrangling. Say black is black, and he'll be delighted to prove, at length, that it is white. Make any statement at all, in fact, and you'll find him upholding the negative, always in an unbearably tedious, and sometimes in a downright quarrelsome, manner. Indeed, agree with him finally, for the sake of peace and quiet, and he will, of course, reverse his previous position, for he is unhappy if he cannot continue the argument.

Call such a person *contentious* and you've picked the exact word that describes him.

DEFINITION

Contentious means: unduly argumentative, excessively disputatious, tediously persistent in dispute.

PRONUNCIATIONS

Contentious	kən-TEN'-shəs
Contentiousness	kən-TEN'-shəs-nəs

DERIVATION

Latin *contendo,* to struggle.

Check Your Learning

I. TRUE OR FALSE?

1. *Indolence* is characteristic of energetic people.	True	False
2. *Intransigence* is complete unwillingness to compromise.	True	False
3. *Contrition* is a happy feeling.	True	False
4. *Puerility* indicates retarded maturity.	True	False
5. *Contentiousness* makes for popularity.	True	False

II. SAME OR OPPOSITE?

1. Indolent—ambitious	Same	Opposite
2. Intransigent—flexible	Same	Opposite
3. Contrite—contented	Same	Opposite
4. Puerile—callow	Same	Opposite
5. Contentious—belligerent	Same	Opposite

III. USE THE WORD

1. Marie was a deep, mature woman, but her husband was given to such _____ behavior that we wondered whether they had a true man-and-woman, or a mother-and-son relationship.
2. He felt so _____ over the way he had treated his son that his guilt made it impossible for him to react normally.
3. He's the most _____ person we've ever met; he seems to spend most of his life doing absolutely nothing.
4. You'll never get him to agree to any change in party policy; on questions of politics he's a complete _____.
5. What a _____ bore! He's one man I'm never going to get into an argument with.

IV. WRITE THE WORD

1. Tediously and persistently argumentative   1. _____
2. Penitent over a misdeed   2. _____
3. Immature and annoyingly childish   3. _____
4. Lazy, lacking in drive, ambition, or energy   4. _____
5. Unwilling to compromise or yield   5. _____

Test Your Learning

ANSWERS TO TESTS ON UNIT 4

TEST I
   1—false, 2—true, 3—false, 4—true, 5—false.

TEST II
   1—opposite, 2—opposite, 3—opposite, 4—same, 5—same.

TEST III
   1—puerile, 2—contrite, 3—indolent, 4—intransigent, 5—contentious.

TEST IV
   1—contentious, 2—contrite, 3—puerile, 4—indolent, 5—intransigent.

Review Test I
(A Complete Check on Your Understanding of Words 1–20)

A. CHANGE PARTS OF SPEECH

Change each adjective to the noun that will properly fit into the accompanying phrase.

1. celibate   Vows of _____.
2. frugal   His enforced _____.
3. decorous   A model of _____.

4. docile   Too much _____.

5. iconoclastic   The _____ of adolescence.

6. diffident   An excessive amount of _____.

7. vindictive   Fear of his well-known _____.

8. acerb   His characteristic _____.

9. phlegmatic   The unalterable _____ of his nature.

10. recalcitrant   Unable to handle such _____.

11. verbose   His boring _____.

12. sanctimonious   Such nauseating _____.

13. inane   Disgusted with her _____.

14. dour   (No noun in general use) _____.

15. dogmatic   Unpopular because of his _____.

16. indolent   Laughed at his constant _____.

17. intransigent   His expected _____.

18. contrite   Miserable with _____.

19. puerile   His unbearable _____.

20. contentious   Fed up with her constant _____.

B. SAME OR OPPOSITE?

1. celibate—unmarried	Same	Opposite
2. frugal—extravagant	Same	Opposite
3. decorous—dignified	Same	Opposite
4. docile—recalcitrant	Same	Opposite
5. iconoclastic—conservative	Same	Opposite
6. diffident—shy	Same	Opposite
7. vindictive—retaliatory	Same	Opposite
8. acerb—biting	Same	Opposite
9. phlegmatic—high-strung	Same	Opposite
10. recalcitrant—obedient	Same	Opposite
11. verbose—wordy	Same	Opposite
12. sanctimonious—sincere	Same	Opposite
13. inane—senseless	Same	Opposite
14. dour—pleasure-loving	Same	Opposite
15. dogmatic—positive	Same	Opposite
16. indolent—energetic	Same	Opposite
17. intransigent—inflexible	Same	Opposite
18. contrite—penitent	Same	Opposite
19. puerile—mature	Same	Opposite
20. contentious—argumentative	Same	Opposite

Think of the adjective that has the closest relationship to each key idea. (These are not definitions.)

KEY IDEA	WORD
1. Severity	_____
2. Lack of money	_____
3. Lack of a mate	_____
4. Lack of self-confidence	_____
5. Resistance	_____
6. Controversy	_____
7. Hypocrisy	_____
8. Sharp tongue	_____
9. Lack of compromise	_____
10. Too many words	_____
11. Lack of sense	_____
12. Dignity	_____
13. Immaturity	_____
14. Excessive positiveness	_____
15. Lack of drive	_____
16. Wish for revenge	_____
17. Lack of resistance	_____
18. Pangs of conscience	_____
19. Contempt for conventions	_____
20. Lack of emotionality	_____

D. MATCH WORDS AND MEANINGS

WORDS	MEANINGS
1. celibate	a—obedient
2. frugal	b—seeking revenge
3. decorous	c—unemotional
4. docile	d—severe, harsh, heavy, pleasureless
5. iconoclastic	e—using more words than necessary
6. diffident	f—pointless
7. vindictive	g—excessively positive in utterance of opinions
8. acerb	h—preferring inactivity
9. phlegmatic	i—callow; immature
10. recalcitrant	j—observing conventions of behavior

11. verbose	k—uncompromising
12. sanctimonious	l—unmarried
13. inane	m—tediously argumentative
14. dour	n—regretful of one's misdeeds
15. dogmatic	o—cynical of customs and conventions
16. indolent	p—making a hypocritical pretense of virtue or piousness
17. intransigent	q—economical
18. contrite	r—sharp in speech
19. puerile	s—unmanageable
20. contentious	t—timid because of lack of self-confidence

Check Your Learning

ANSWERS TO REVIEW TEST I

TEST A

1—celibacy, 2—frugality, 3—decorum, 4—docility, 5—iconoclasm, 6—diffidence, 7—vindictiveness, 8—acerbity, 9—phlegmaticness, 10—recalcitrance, 11—verbosity, 12—sanctimony (or sanctimoniousness), 13—inanity, 14—none, 15—dogmatism, 16—indolence, 17—intransigence, 18—contrition, 19—puerility, 20—contentiousness.

TEST B

1—s, 2—o, 3—s, 4—o, 5—o, 6—s, 7—s, 8—s, 9—o, 10—o, 11—s, 12—o, 13—s, 14—o, 15—s, 16—o, 17—s, 18—s, 19—o, 20—s.

TEST C

1—dour, 2—frugal, 3—celibate, 4—diffident, 5—recalcitrant, 6—contentious, 7—sanctimonious, 8—acerb, 9—intransigent, 10—verbose, 11—inane, 12—decorous, 13—puerile, 14—dogmatic, 15—indolent, 16—vindictive, 17—docile, 18—contrite, 19—iconoclastic, 20—phlegmatic.

TEST D

1—l, 2—q, 3—j, 4—a, 5—o, 6—t, 7—b, 8—r, 9—c, 10—s, 11—e, 12—p, 13—f, 14—d, 15—g, 16—h, 17—k, 18—n, 19—i, 20—m.

PART II

Actions

The twenty-five words of Part II are introduced in connection with the Latin root on which each is built.

Here are some of the roots discussed. Can you think of an English verb, ending in either *-fy* or *-ate*, which comes from each root?

amplus	—	large
nullus	—	none
magnus	—	large
os	—	bone
deus	—	god
melior	—	better
robur	—	strength
debilis	—	weak
cras	—	tomorrow
fulmen	—	thunder
juvenis	—	young man
facilis	—	easy

Read on . . .

Unit Five

The ending -fy, found on scores of English verbs, comes indirectly from a Latin root *facio, to make.*

With the help offered in the following test, see how many verbs you can complete.

21. **Amplus** is a Latin word meaning *large, abundant.* (Our adjective *ample* is derived from this root.) What English verb, therefore, means to enlarge upon something by discussion, by giving more particulars, etc. A_____fy

22. **Nullus** is the Latin adjective for *none.* What English verb, therefore, means to render of no value, to make useless? N_____fy

23. **Petra** is the Latin for *rock* or *stone.* What English verb, therefore, means to turn into stone? P_____fy

24. **Vilis** is the Latin for *cheap, vile, base.* What English verb, therefore, means to debase, to accuse of vile deeds? V_____fy

25. **Magnus** is the Latin for *big.* What English verb, therefore, means to exaggerate, make appear larger than in actuality? M_____fy

26. **Os** is the Latin for *bone.* What English verb, therefore, means to turn into bone? O_____fy

27. **Mollis,** in Latin, means *soft.* What English verb, therefore, means to soften, figuratively speaking; that is, to appease, smooth over someone's hostility? M_____fy

28. **Stupere** is a Latin verb meaning *to stun.* What English verb, therefore, means to deprive of sensibility or to shock greatly? S_____fy

29. **Putrere,** in Latin, means *to rot.* What English verb, therefore, means to become rotten, to decompose? P_____fy

30. **Deus** is the Latin noun for *God*. What English verb, therefore, means to make a god of, to worship like a god, to treat as an object of supreme worship?   D_____fy

ANSWERS

You notice, in this Unit, how English words are directly built on Latin roots. These are only ten of a score of words containing the suffix *-fy* from the Latin verb *facio*, to make; other examples are *clarify*, to make clear, from Latin *clarus; diversify*, to make of varied nature, from Latin *diversus; pacify*, to make peaceful, to calm, from Latin *pax; rectify*, to make right, to correct, from Latin *rectus*, etc. Check your results now with the answers below, and notice how each word is used, how it changes into various forms, how it is pronounced, and what its deeper connotations are.

21. **Amplify** (AM'-plə-fī'). Someone may ask you to *amplify* your remarks, or to *amplify* a statement. In answer to such a request, you give more details, examples, or explanations: in other words you enlarge upon the basic concept of what you have said. You *amplify* something which, as it stands, is inadequate in size, power, or force, or is insufficiently clear. You may, for example, use a device to *amplify* sound. The noun is *amplification*, as in "We need an *amplification* of your ideas before we can understand them." The adjective is *ample*, which has the simple meaning of *enough*, as in "He had an *ample* breakfast."

22. **Nullify** (NUL'-ə-fī'). If you *nullify* a contract or agreement, you render it void and inoperative; if an action of yours *nullifies* the previous good you have done, it serves to take away the value of previous good actions. The noun is *nullification*.

23. **Petrify** (PET'-rə-fī'). Slowly, through the ages, wood *petrifies;* it becomes stone. In the figurative phrase "*petrified* with fear," the implication is that the fright is so tremendous that one is paralyzed, practically turned into stone. The noun is *petrifaction*.

24. **Vilify** (ViL'-ə-fī'). You *vilify* someone by calling him vile names, by slandering him, by accusing him (often publicly) of low, mean, base acts or motives. The noun is *vilification*.

25. **Magnify** (MAG'-nə-fī'). Place a *magnifying* lens over an object and you will understand clearly what this verb means: what you are looking at *seems* considerably bigger, though in actuality it is the same size. So if you *magnify* your troubles, you view them

as greater than they are; if you *magnify* someone's importance, you overrate his value, etc. The noun is *magnification* (a microscope has several degrees of *magnification*—that is, it can show an object in various sizes) or *magnitude*, which means great size (a star of the first *magnitude* is very bright). "*Magnitude* of mind" refers to moral greatness, and in the sentence "He scarcely could realize the *magnitude* of his loss" the implication is that the immensity of his loss was beyond his comprehension.

26. **Ossify** (OS'-ə-fī'). When part of the body *ossifies*, it turns into bone, or hardens like bone. During the normal course of growth, various tissues form into bone, or go through a process of *ossification*. And then there is the slang term *ossified*, meaning greatly intoxicated, which is simply a poetic exaggeration.

27. **Mollify** (MOL'-ə-fī'). By kind words, by gracious acts or winning ways, you attempt to *mollify* someone who is insulted, angry, hostile, annoyed, etc. If such a peron is beyond *mollification*, there is no possibility of appeasing his anger, of reducing his hostility.

28. **Stupefy** (STOO'-pə-fī'). To *stupefy* someone is to shock or stun him to such a degree, figuratively speaking, as to render him incapable of using his faculties; in other words to astound him, to overwhelm him with amazement. More literally, *stupefaction* can be brought about by a narcotic, by alcohol, by great emotional shock, by physical accident, etc. In such a case, the faculties of the victim actually do become numb, insensible, unable to function.

29. **Putrefy** (PYOO'-trə-fī'). Any animal substance which is cut off from its blood supply will *putrefy*, that is decay, or rot. When we speak of the odor of *putrefaction*, we refer to that offensive smell which usually accompanies animal decay.

30. **Deify** (DEE'-ə-fī'). When you *deify* someone, you set him up as a god, you worship him with that blind intensity usually reserved for a supreme being. Some people tend to *deify* business superiors, movie stars, political leaders, teachers, etc. The noun is *deification*.

PRONUNCIATIONS

Amplify—AM'-plə-fī'
Amplification—am'-plə-fə-KAY'-shən
Nullify—NUL'-ə-fī'
Nullification—null'-ə-fə-KAY'-shən

Petrify—PET'-rə-fī'
Petrifaction—pet'-rə-FAK'-shən
Vilify—VIL'-ə-fī'
Vilification—vill'-ə-fə-KAY'-shən
Magnify—MAG'-nə-fī'
Magnification—mag'-nə-fə-KAY'-shən
Ossify—OS'-ə-fī'
Ossification—os'-ə-fə-KAY'-shən
Mollify—MOL'-ə-fī'
Mollification—mol'-ə-fə-KAY'-shən
Stupefy—STOO-pə-fī'
Stupefaction—stoo-pə-FAK'-shən
Putrefy—PYOO-trə-fī'
Putrefaction—pyoo-trə-FAK'-shən
Deify—DEE'-ə-fī'
Deification—dee'-ə-fə-KAY'-shən

SPELLING CAUTIONS

Notice that in most words ending in -*fy*, the suffix is preceded by the vowel *i*. However, in *putrefy* and *stupefy*, an *e* precedes the -*fy*. An *e* is also found in the verb liqu*e*fy. All this, despite the fact that the adjective forms contain an *i*: putr*i*d, stup*i*d, liqu*i*d.

Be careful of these:

1. *putrefy*, not *putrify*
2. *stupefy*, not *stupify*
3. *liquefy*, not *liquify*

Test Your Learning

I. MATCH WORDS WITH MEANINGS

WORDS	MEANINGS
1. amplify	a—turn to stone
2. nullify	b—turn to bone
3. petrify	c—astound; paralyze
4. vilify	d—treat as a god
5. magnify	e—slander, accuse of base deeds
6. ossify	f—enlarge upon
7. mollify	g—appease
8. stupefy	h—make seem larger than in actuality
9. putrefy	i—rot
10. deify	j—render void

APPLY THE WORDS

Choose the concept from column B to which each verb in column A would most logically apply.

A	B
1. amplify	a—with fear
2. nullify	b—corpse
3. petrify	c—one's troubles
4. vilify	d—one's leader
5. magnify	e—with amazement
6. ossify	f—a statement
7. mollify	g—bodily tissue
8. stupefy	h—a political opponent
9. putrefy	i—someone who is angry
10. deify	j—a contract

III. YES OR NO?

1. If someone asks you to *amplify* your statement, do you give more details?   *Yes   No*
2. If a contract has been *nullified,* is it still in force?   *Yes   No*
3. When wood *petrifies*, does it become soft and pulpy?   *Yes   No*
4. If you indulge in *vilification*, are you kind, courteous, and considerate?   *Yes   No*
5. If you *magnify* your troubles, are you being realistic?   *Yes   No*
6. Do parts of an infants' anatomy eventually *ossify?*   *Yes   No*
7. If you succeed in *mollifying* someone you've offended, does he then feel friendlier toward you?   *Yes   No*
8. Is a person who is *stupefied* with astonishment able to think with great clarity?   *Yes   No*
9. Is tissue which has been cut off from its blood supply in danger of *putrefaction?*   *Yes   No*
10. Did many people in Germany once tend to *deify* Hitler?   *Yes   No*

IV. CHANGE PARTS OF SPEECH

Change each of the following verbs into a noun that will properly fit into the accompanying phrase.

1. Amplify   The _____ of sound
2. Nullify   The _____ of his plans
3. Petrify   The _____ of wood
4. Vilify   His _____ of his opponent
5. Magnify   The _____ of his troubles
6. Ossify   _____ of tissue taking place

7. Mollify   Counting on the _____ of his enemy
8. Stupefy   His complete _____
9. Putrefy   The _____ of unrefrigerated meat
10. Deify   The _____ of their leader

V. WRITE THE WORD

Write the verb we have studied that fits each definition.

1. To smooth over   _____
2. To turn to stone   _____
3. To become rotten   _____
4. To treat like a god   _____
5. To make larger or completer   _____
6. To render void   _____
7. To turn to bone   _____
8. To accuse of base deeds   _____
9. To stun with amazement   _____
10. To make seem larger than in actuality   _____

Check Your Learning

ANSWERS TO TEST ON UNIT 5

TEST I

1—f, 2—j, 3—a, 4—e, 5—h, 6—b, 7—g, 8—c, 9—i, 10—d.

TEST II

1—f, 2—j, 3—a, 4—h, 5—c, 6—g, 7—i, 8—e, 9—b, 10—d.

TEST III

1—yes, 2—no, 3—no, 4—no, 5—no, 6—yes, 7—yes, 8—no, 9—yes, 10—yes.

TEST IV

1—amplification, 2—nullification, 3—petrifaction, 4—vilification, 5—magnification, 6—ossification, 7—mollification, 8—stupefaction, 9—putrefaction, 10—deification.

TEST V

1—mollify, 2—petrify, 3—putrefy, 4—deify, 5—amplify, 6—nullify, 7—ossify, 8—vilify, 9—stupefy, 10—magnify.

Unit Six

With the help offered in the following test, see how many verbs you can complete.

This, keep in mind, is not a test of your learning nor of your knowledge; it is intended only as a means of stimulating your interest in the words to be discussed. So complete each verb if you can; and if you cannot, refer to the key following the test. The less successful you are, as it happens, the more valuable this unit will be for you.

31. **Melior** is a Latin adjective meaning *better*. What English verb, therefore, means to make better, to improve upon?

    A_____ate

32. **Captivus** is the Latin noun for *captive*. What English verb, therefore, means to fascinate, to charm, to acquire power over by art, allurements, or attraction, in short to take captive, figuratively speaking?

    C_____ate

33. **Castigare** is a Latin root meaning *to correct*. What English verb, therefore, means to criticize harshly, reprove severely, give a tongue-lashing to?

    C_____ate

34. **Robur** is a Latin root meaning *strength*. What English verb, therefore, means, literally, to give strength to; or, by extension, to confirm or give added support to a statement, an opinion, an item of evidence, etc.?

    C_____ate

35. **Debilis** is a Latin adjective meaning *weak*. What English verb, therefore, means to enfeeble, impair the strength of, remove vigor or well-being?

    D_____ate

ANSWERS

31. **Ameliorate** (ə-MEEL'-yə-rayt'). An excellent word, but one that must be used with care. In its proper pattern, *ameliorate* has great force and, as will be detailed shortly, a unique connotation, but

47

bear in mind that it cannot be substituted indiscriminately for its synonym *to improve*. You can *improve* a person, a thing, a state, or a condition, by making some corrections for changes, and no matter whether such person, thing, state, or condition was good or bad. But you *ameliorate* conditions exclusively, and only when they are unbearable or productive of suffering or hardship. Thus, you can improve a man's vocabulary, his golf score, his character, his economic condition, or his attitude to his wife. You *ameliorate* his condition when he is in great pain (perhaps by the injection of morphine); you *ameliorate* the conditions of poverty-stricken refugees (by sanitation, better food, new housing, etc.); or you *ameliorate* the conditions under which convicts live in certain prisons (by installing recreation rooms, improving the food, etc.). The noun is *amelioration*, generally followed by the preposition *of*, as in the phrases "Devoted himself to the *amelioration* of the condition of clients on relief," "Intended for the *amelioration* of the living conditions of prisoners," etc.

32. **Captivate** (KAP'-tə-vayt'). You *capture* someone by taking physical possession of his person; you *captivate* him by taking possession, in a sense, of his feelings or fancy, by appealing to his emotions by means of charm, delightfulness, attractiveness, beauty, wit, etc. A singer's charm *captivates* an audience; a child's merriment *captivates* those adults who relate well to children and laughter; the virile-looking life guard at a summer resort *captivates* all the romantic maidens. The adjective is *captivating*, as in "a *captivating* smile," a "*captivating* child."

33. **Castigate** (KAS-tə-gayt'). To *castigate* someone is to criticize and rebuke him, usually publicly, with the harshest of language, either spoken or written. We may speak of "A *castigating* attack on a political opponent," "A defendant's *castigation*, in court, of the arresting officer," or "The judge who *castigated* unmercifully all the gamblers who came before him."

34. **Corroborate** (kə-ROB'-ə-rayt'). To *corroborate* is to make a statement which someone else has made. Never the person himself, but only what he has said (or written) is *corroborated*. An objective fact may also *corroborate*. For example, a man claims that women dress only to please the male sex. At that moment his wife enters the room, wearng a new dress. "Do you like it?" she asks her husband. "Absolutely not! It looks terrible," he answers. "Really?" she says, "I thought it made me look attractive." "Not a bit," says her husband, "I don't like it at all." "Oh, in that case I'll

take it right back to the store." When his wife leaves, the man has a knowing look. "See?" he says, "*That* corroborates my statement."

The following are the general patterns in which *corroborate* and its forms are used:

"He offered *corroborating* evidence to support his claims."

"He offered new evidence in *corroboration* of his claims."

"She *corroborated*, without qualification, everything he had said."

"My statement is further *corroborated* by scientific investigations at the Mayo Clinic."

"Your statement *corroborates* an opinion I had privately formed."

35. **Debilitate** (də-BIL′-ə-tayt′). An illness which temporarily weakens a person, robbing him of ambition, energy, and normal vigor, may be called a *debilitating* illness. A very hot, muggy climate may similarly affect people, and would then correctly be called a *debilitating* climate. Any condition or circumstance, then, which saps a person's physical strength is *debilitating*. We may also say that the fighter, *debilitated* by a long life of dissipation, was no match for his younger and fresher opponent, or that long weeks of carousing and drinking have *debilitated* the fighter. The noun is *debilitation*.

PRONUNCIATIONS

Ameliorate—ə-MEEL′-yə-rayt′
Captivate—KAP′-tə-vayt′
Castigate—KAS′-tə-gayt′
Corroborate—kə-ROB′-ə-rayt′
Debilitate—də-BIL′-ə-tayt′

SPELLING CAUTION

Corroborate contains a double *r* near the beginning, a single *r* toward the end.

Test Your Learning

I. TRUE OR FALSE?

1. If conditions under which the prisoners live are *ameliorated*, prison existence becomes more bearable.   *True*   *False*

2. A sulky, contentious, dogmatic person is likely to *captivate* an audience.   *True*   *False*

3. Most people enjoy being *castigated*.   *True*   *False*
4. *Corroborating* evidence weakens a claim.   *True*   *False*
5. Prolonged dissipation has a *debilitating* effect.   *True*   *False*

II. SAME OR OPPOSITE?

1. Ameliorate—improve   *Same*   *Opposite*
2. Captivate—alienate   *Same*   *Opposite*
3. Castigate—commend   *Same*   *Opposite*
4. Corroborate—deny   *Same*   *Opposite*
5. Debilitate—enfeeble   *Same*   *Opposite*

III. USE THE WORD

1. He had just recovered from a _____ illness, and looked pale and listless.
2. Her _____ smile immediately won her audience.
3. Certain principles have been agreed to by most nations for the _____ of the conditions of war prisoners.
4. She delivered a _____ attack upon her husband, and, strangely enough, the all-male jury listened sympathetically.
5. What you have just said completely _____ what I have always thought.

IV. WRITE THE WORD

1. To censure, rebuke, or attack verbally and with great harshness   1. _____
2. To confirm, or give added support to a statement   2. _____
3. To improve (conditions)   3. _____
4. To weaken physically   4. _____
5. To win over, charm, attract   5. _____

Check Your Learning

ANSWERS TO TESTS ON UNIT 6

TEST I

1—true, 2—false, 3—false, 4—false, 5—true.

TEST II

1—same, 2—opposite, 3—opposite, 4—opposite, 5—same.

TEST III

1—debilitating, 2—captivating, 3—amelioration, 4—castigating, 5—corroborates.

TEST IV

1—castigate, 2—corroborate, 3—ameliorate, 4—debilitate, 5—captivate.

Unit Seven

Again, with the hints offered in the preliminary test, see how many of the five words of this unit you can correctly fill in.

36. **Praeceps** is a Latin adverb meaning *headlong*. What English verb, therefore, means to make happen suddenly or unexpectedly, or (to tie the word up to the root from which it originates) to cause an event to plunge headlong into existence?   P_____ate

37. **Valere** is a Latin verb that means *to be well* or *strong*. What English verb, therefore, means to render null and void, to weaken the force or value of?   I_____ate

38. **Pontiff** is a synonym for the highest officer of the Roman Catholic church, and probably comes from the Latin roots *pons, bridge,* and *facio, make.* (In a figurative sense, the pope is a person who points the path of righteousness, builds the bridge to morality, etc.) What English verb, therefore, means to talk as if one were the pope (even though one isn't), that is, in an unusually dignified and authoritive manner?   P_____ate

39. **Litera** is the Latin noun for *letter* or *writing*. What English verb, therefore, means to erase writing, or, in an extended sense, destroy completely?   O_____ate

40. **Iterum** is the Latin adverb meaning *again*. What English verb, therefore, means to say again, to repeat?   R_____ate

36. **Precipitate** (prə-SIP′-ə-tayt′). If you *precipitate* an event, a circumstance, or a reaction (the only things you *can* precipitate), you bring it on suddenly, unexpectedly, before it is due, and often when it is not desirable. For example, a normal pregnancy takes, as almost everyone knows in these days of enlightenment, nine full months, give or take a few days. However, any unusual physical activity, or certain drugs or cathartics, will *precipitate* labor—that is, make labor start before it is due, perhaps before it is advisable. Again, nations may be indulging in a so-called "cold war," perhaps before they are ready to start shooting, possibly in the hopes of eventually avoiding warfare altogether. But some act of aggression, some overstepping of the bounds on the part of one of the nations may suddenly, even prematurely, change "cold" to "hot" . . . this act has *precipitated* war. Similarly, you can *precipitate* an argument, a quarrel, a battle, someone's resignation from a business firm (he may have been planning tentatively to resign but was not yet completely decided), expulsion from a college, and so on.

37. **Invalidate** (in-VAL′-ə-dayt′). *Invalidate* something and you make it no longer valid—you make it nonoperative or prove that it is not true or rob it of its force, power, or legality. A Supreme Court opinion can *invalidate* a local or state law which the Justices deem contrary to the U.S. Constitution; or, to descend considerably in the scale of values, tearing a coupon out of a book of railroad tickets *invalidates* it, that is, makes it unusable, though actually few train conductors have the time or interest to become technical about the matter. In some wills, if a beneficiary contests the provisions, his action *invalidates* the document—renders it null and void as far as he is concerned. Or a certain complex theory is built up, step by step, each part growing from the previous part. Then someone proves that one of the early steps is untrue, does not square with facts. Such proof *invalidates* the entire theory.

38. **Pontificate** (pon-TIF′-ə-kayt′). The pope, since he is the pope, naturally expresses his opinions with the dignity, ceremony, and authority which his supreme office confers upon him. When a lesser mortal attempts to talk in the same manner about the same eternal values, almost as if he were a supreme, divinely inspired authority, it doesn't quite come off, naturally. Such solemnity

simply seems ludicrous, conceited, absurd. So we may say, in derogation, that this lesser mortal is *pontificating. Pontificate,* an excellent word for which there are no close synonyms, is always used to show contempt; a *pontificator* speaks with an air of self-importance to which he is not entitled.

39. **Obliterate** (əb-LIT′-ə-rayt′). Originally, *obliterate* meant *erase,* just as you turn your pencil around and erase what you have written. Such an act completely removes the writing—hence the present meaning of the verb, to do something which completely removes every trace of a thing's existence. A heavy snowstorm can *obliterate* the highway; a second marriage can *obliterate* all memory of the first mate; a man's success in a new venture can *obliterate* past failures; and a heavy aerial bombing can attempt to *obliterate* a village, a munitions dump, a factory, etc.

40. **Reiterate** (ree-IT′-ə-rayt′). *Reiterate* means, of course, to repeat, but there is an important distinction. You may repeat anything— a success, a failure, a statement, a movement, an action, and so on. To *reiterate,* on the other hand, always implies the repetition of *words,* or of an idea by means of words; furthermore, such reiteration is for the purpose of emphasis or insistence. "I reiterate," says the candidate, "that my worthy opponent is a fool, a scoundrel, and a thief." The candidate has made the point before and makes it again, because he wants you to remember it and believe it.

PRONUNCIATIONS

Precipitate—prə-SIP′-ə-tayt′
Invalidate—in-VAL′-ə-dayt′
Pontificate—pont-TIF′-ə-kayt′
Obliterate—əb-LIT′-ə-rayt′
Reiterate—ree-IT′-ə-rayt′

USAGE CAUTIONS

1. Only an event, circumstance, reaction, or the like can be *precipitated.*
2. You *invalidate* a document, a law, a theory, an opinion, etc.—never a person, fact, or occurrence.
3. *Pontificate* refers to speech, language, or writing.
4. You *obliterate* a place, a memory, a thing—but not a person.
5. To *reiterate* is to repeat a word, a phrase, or (in words) an idea or opinion.

Test Your Learning

I. TRUE OR FALSE?

1. Insults can *precipitate* a quarrel.   True   False
2. A contrary set of actual facts can *invalidate* a theory.   True   False
3. People who *pontificate* are usually modest and diffident.   True   False
4. If you *obliterate* something, none of it remains.   True   False
5. If you *reiterate* a phrase, you say it only once.   True   False

II. SAME OR OPPOSITE?

1. Precipitate—delay   Same   Opposite
2. Invalidate—nullify   Same   Opposite
3. Pontificate—speak triflingly   Same   Opposite
4. Obliterate—reinforce   Same   Opposite
5. Reiterate—repeat   Same   Opposite

III. USE THE WORD

1. Over and over he had heard the lie ＿＿＿＿＿ and so he had finally come to believe it.
2. His violent temper has ＿＿＿＿＿ many an unnecessary quarrel.
3. He doesn't just talk—he ＿＿＿＿＿ ; who does he think he is, anyway?
4. Through hypnosis, all memory of the pain and misery was ＿＿＿＿＿ .
5. These new discoveries will ＿＿＿＿＿ all earlier and contrary theories.

IV. WRITE THE WORD

1. To remove every trace of   1. ＿＿＿＿＿
2. To render null and void   2. ＿＿＿＿＿
3. To repeat for emphasis   3. ＿＿＿＿＿
4. To make happy suddenly and unexpectedly   4. ＿＿＿＿＿
5. To talk in an excessively solemn, dignified, and self-important manner   5. ＿＿＿＿＿

Check Your Learning

ANSWERS TO TESTS ON UNIT SEVEN

TEST I

   1—true, 2—true, 3—false, 4—true, 5—false.

TEST II

   1—opposite, 2—same, 3—opposite, 4—opposite, 5—same.

TEST III

1—reiterated, 2—precipitated, 3—pontificates, 4—obliterated,
5—invalidate.

TEST IV

1—obliterate, 2—invalidate, 3—reiterate, 4—precipitate,
5—pontificate.

Unit Eight

Here are five more verbs ending in *-ate*, with the usual explanations as to roots and origins, and another chance to see how many you can successfully complete.

41. **Capacis** is the adjective form of the Latin verb *capere, to take*. What English verb, therefore, means to deprive of ability, to disable?

    1. I_____ate

42. **Cras** is the Latin adverb meaning *tomorrow*. What English verb, therefore, means literally to put off till tomorrow, in other words to delay, to make a habit of postponing actions or decisions?

    2. P_____ate

43. **Fulmen** is a Latin noun meaning *thunderbolt*. What English verb, therefore, means to thunder forth with criticism, violent verbal attacks, threats, denunciations, etc.?

    3. F_____ate

44. **Juvenis** is a Latin noun meaning *a young man*. What English verb, therefore, means to make youthful again, to reinvigorate?

    4. R_____ate

45. **Facile** is a Latin adjective meaning *easy*. What English verb, therefore, means to make easy, render less difficult?

    5. F_____ate

ANSWERS

41. **Incapacitate** (in′-kə-PAS′-ə-tayt′). Break your arm, through an unfortunate accident, and you can still get around and perhaps even do your work (unless, of course, you are a baseball pitcher, a violinist, or a practitioner or some other art which requires the use of a good right arm)—you are not truly *incapacitated*. A

broken leg is considerably more *incapacitating,* and an illness which lays you flat on your back until you recover *incapacitates* you completely. Generally, to *incapacitate* means to remove physical ability to perform one's regular duties and tasks, but we may also speak of someone being mentally *incapacitated* by a deep neurosis, a brain injury, great shock, or fear.

42. **Procrastinate** (prō-KRAS′-tə-nayt′). Despite the copybook maxim, few normal human beings are prompt in the performance of necessary, but uninteresting, tasks. "Never put off till tomorrow what you can do today," says the maxim, but most of us delay from day to day, or wait till the last possible moment to perform, those duties we find irksome. It is, in short, only human to *procrastinate.* The habitual delayer is a *procrastinator.*

43. **Fulminate** (FUL′-mə-nayt′). Perhaps the best way to appreciate this word fully is to think of Muammar Qaddafi, the Libyan strongman. When he denounces his enemies it is as if Jupiter were hurling thunderbolts at defenseless mortals. The intemperateness of the language, the violence, the explosiveness, the noise, the vehemence of the threats and accusations—such qualities can be described by no less a word than *fulminations.* Qaddafi often *fulminates* against those who irritate or oppose him, as also does the Ayatollah Khomeini, and as similarly did Adolf Hitler, though no other correspondence between these gentlemen is here intended. *Fulminations* are, of course, never gentle or sweetly persuasive—they are, on the contrary, full of sound and fury and as noisy, figuratively speaking, as true thunder. The verb *fulminate* is always followed by the preposition *against,* and the word, or any of its forms, always refers to speech or writing.

44. **Rejuvenate** (rə-JOO′-və-nayt′). Some people believe that drugs, hormones, or vitamins have the power to rejuvenate the aging— to restore them to youthful vigor and freshness, to make them young again. Anything *rejuvenates* which gives to an older person the powers of youth, or even the appearance of youth. These powers or this appearance may be quite temporary or, on the contrary, long-lasting. You have perhaps heard someone say, on waking from a nap, "I feel completely *rejuvenated.*"

45. **Facilitate** (fə-SIL′-ə-tayt′). When you *facilitate* an activity, you offer, or use, some means of making it less arduous, less difficult, in short easier. The preparation of infants' foods has been greatly *facilitated* by precooked cereals, strained baby foods in sealed jars, minced meat, etc. Formerly, cereal had to be cooked for

hours, vegetables had to be painfully pressed through a fine strainer, meats had to be chopped, cumbersomely, by hand. (Indeed, modern science has *facilitated* every aspect of child rearing, including the actual birth and delivery.) Make any work, task, action, etc., easier, simpler, quicker, and you *facilitate* it.

PRONUNCIATIONS

Incapacitate—in′-kə-PAS′-ə-tayt′
Procrastinate—prō-KRAS′-tə-nayt′
Fulminate—FUL′-mə-nayt′ (The first syllable rhymes with *dull*, not *bull*.)
Rejuvenate—rə-JOO′-və-nayt′
Facilitate—fə-SIL′-ə-tayt′

USAGE CAUTIONS

1. Only a *person* is *incapacitated*—and while the *incapacity* may be physical or mental, the verb is generally preceded by *mentally* if the *incapacity* is of the mind.
2. A person *procrastinates*—the verb is not followed by an object.
3. *Fulmination* refers to language, spoken or written. *Fulminate* is always followed by *against*.
4. Generally, only a person is *rejuvenated*.
5. An activity, task, etc., is *facilitated*.

Test Your Learning

I. TRUE OR FALSE?

1. A completely paralyzed person is *incapacitated*.	True	False
2. Only the rare individual never *procrastinates*.	True	False
3. People of violent temper are likely to *fulminate* against those who anger or oppose them.	True	False
4. Ponce de Leon, searching for the Fountain of Youth, was looking for a *rejuvenating* agent.	True	False
5. If you *facilitate* someone's departure, you make it difficult for him to leave.	True	False

II. SAME OR OPPOSITE?

1. Incapacitate—disable	Same	Opposite
2. Procrastinate—delay	Same	Opposite

3. Fulminate—protest gently   *Same*   *Opposite*
4. Rejuvenate—age   *Same*   *Opposite*
5. Facilitate—make easy   *Same*   *Opposite*

III. USE THE WORD

1. This new machine greatly _____ our work.
2. The accident _____ him for several weeks.
3. His work was never in on time—he was a habitual _____.
4. New drugs are constantly being tested for the _____ of older people.
5. The Republicans generally _____ against the Democrats when the latter are in power—and, of course, vice versa.

IV. WRITE THE WORD

1. To delay   1. _____
2. To thunder against in criticism or censure   2. _____
3. To make easier   3. _____
4. To disable   4. _____
5. To make young again   5. _____

Check Your Learning

ANSWERS TO TESTS ON UNIT 8

TEST I

    1—true, 2—true, 3—true, 4—true, 5—false.

TEST II

    1—same, 2—same, 3—opposite, 4—opposite, 5—same.

TEST III

    1—facilitates, 2—incapacitated, 3—procrastinator, 4—rejuvenation, 4—fulminate.

TEST IV

    1—procrastinate, 2—fulminate, 3—facilitate, 4—incapacitate, 5—rejuvenate.

Review Test II

(A Complete Check on Your Understanding of Words 21–45)

A. SAME OR OPPOSITE?

1. amplify—reduce   *Same*   *Opposite*
2. nullify—invalidate   *Same*   *Opposite*
3. vilify—deify   *Same*   *Opposite*

4. mollify—irritate	Same	Opposite
5. ameliorate—improve	Same	Opposite
6. captivate—charm	Same	Opposite
7. castigate—scold	Same	Opposite
8. corroborate—deny	Same	Opposite
9. debilitate—rejuvenate	Same	Opposite
10. precipitate—delay	Same	Opposite
11. obliterate—erase	Same	Opposite
12. reiterate—repeat	Same	Opposite
13. incapacitate—invigorate	Same	Opposite
14. procrastinate—defer	Same	Opposite
15. fulminate against—vilify	Same	Opposite
16. facilitate—hinder	Same	Opposite

B. USE THE VERB

From column I choose the verb that most effectively completes the pattern of each phrase in Column II.

I	II
1. corroborate	a—to _____ his audience
2. precipitate	b—to _____ when the task is unpleasant
3. magnify	c—to _____ with amazement
4. ameliorate	d—to _____ the task
5. captivate	e—to _____ the statement
6. stupefy	f—to _____ against the enemies
7. fulminate	g—to _____ all memory
8. procrastinate	h—to _____ an argument
9. facilitate	i—to _____ conditions
10. obliterate	j—to _____ his troubles

C FIND THE MEANING

From Column II, choose the verb which best fits each meaning in column I.

I	II
1. Turn to stone	a—vilify
2. Turn to bone	b—deify
3. Become rotten	c—putrefy
4. Slander; hurl accusations at	d—amplify
5. Smooth over; make peaceful	e—nullify
6. Treat like a god	f—ossify
7. Elaborate upon; increase the volume of	g—captivate

60

8. Render valueless
9. Charm; attract
10. Weaken

h—mollify
i—debilitate
j—petrify

D. CHOOSE A VERB

Check the verb which most closely fits each definition.

1. To scold harshly
   a—invalidate, b—castigate, c—rejuvenate.
2. Make useless
   a—pontificate, b—reiterate, c—invalidate.
3. To give the power or appearance of youth
   a—facilitate, b—incapacitate, c—rejuvenate.
4. To talk with excessive ceremony or absurd self-importance
   a—pontificate, b—fulminate, c—ameliorate.
5. To repeat for further emphasis
   a—procrastinate, b—facilitate, c—reiterate.

E. THINK OF THE VERB

1. Make easier	1. F	
2. Put out of commission	2. I	
3. Weaken	3. D	
4. Make seem larger than in actuality	4. M	
5. Render ineffective	5. N	
6. Improve	6. A	
7. Thunder against	7. F	
8. Make happen suddenly	8. P	
9. Make young again	9. R	
10. Render null and void	10. I	
11. Delay	11. P	
12. Support	12. C	
13. Give more details	13. A	
14. Stun with surprise	14. S	
15. Scold severely	15. C	
16. Charm	16. C	
17. Turn to stone	17. P	
18. Turn to bone	18. O	
19. Repeat	20. R	
20. Remove all traces of	20. O	
21. Worship as a god	21. D	
22. Accuse of low and base deeds or motives	22. V	

23. Appease; change hostility to friend-
    liness
24. Talk with excessive dignity
25. Rot

23. M_____

24. P_____

25. P_____

Check Your Learning

ANSWERS TO REVIEW TEST II

TEST A

1—opposite, 2—same, 3—opposite, 4—opposite, 5—same, 6—same, 7—
same, 8—opposite, 9—opposite, 10—opposite, 11—same, 12—same, 13—
opposite, 14—same, 15—same, 16—opposite.

TEST B

a—5, b—8, c—6, d—9, e—1, f—7, g—10, h—2, i—4, j—3.

TEST C

1—j, 2—f, 3—c, 4—a, 5—h, 6—b, 7—d, 8—e, 9—g, 10—i.

TEST D

1—b, 2—c, 3—c, 4—a, 5—c.

TEST E

1—facilitate, 2—incapacitate, 3—debilitate, 4—magnify, 5—nullify, 6—
ameliorate, 7—fulminate (against), 8—precipitate, 9—rejuvenate, 10—invalidate, 11—procrastinate, 12—corroborate, 13—amplify, 14—stupefy, 15—
castigate, 16—captivate, 17—petrify, 18—ossify, 19—reiterate, 20—obliterate, 21—deify, 22—vilify, 23—mollify, 24—pontificate, 25—putrefy.

PART III

Roots

The twenty words in Part III are also introduced in connection with the Latin or Greek roots from which they derive.

Here is a list of some of the roots discussed. Can you think of an English word which is built on each root?

Nascor—to be born
Moneo—to warn
Claudo—to close
Phobia—fear
Cupio—to desire
Pedis—foot
Haero—to stick
Fortis—strong

Read on . . .

Unit Nine

A large part of our English vocabulary comes from Latin or Greek words. The core of our language is of course Anglo-Saxon (which, in turn, is a Teutonic tongue, and therefore directly related to German), and basic, everyday words like *mother, father, sister, brother, cow, sheep, pig, house, love, life, death*, etc. are of Anglo-Saxon origin. Most abstract words, however, those that describe intangible feelings, deep ideas, the life of thought and emotional reactions, are built on roots we have taken from either Latin or Greek.

Look around you, and name the concrete objects you see—the words are likely to be short, simple, and Anglo-Saxon. Then start analyzing how people act, how they feel, how they think, and you will probably couch your ideas very largely in words of more than one syllable, in terms built on Latin or Greek roots.

We shall explore some of these roots and the English words springing from them in the four units of Part III.

46. PRENATAL

If an English word begins with *pre-*, the likelihood is that there is some connotation of "beforeness" in it, for most such words combine some Latin root with the Latin prefix *prae*, which means *before*. [*Prefix* itself is one such example: A *prefix* is a syllable *fixed before* a root to form a word, such as *in*, meaning *not* (*in*correct, *in*capable); *contra*, meaning *against*, (*contra*dict); *bi*, meaning *two* (*bi*cycle, *bi*sect).]

The Latin preposition *prae*, *before*, is usually spelled *pre* in English words; and if you are immediately aware of the meaning of "beforeness" that *pre-* lends to words, you will have little trouble understanding terms that contain this common beginning.

Consider, for a moment, a Latin verb which means *to be born: nascor, nasci, natus*. (Most Latin verbs have three or four forms, and an English word may be built on any of them, as we shall shortly see.)

Very often, the syllable *nasc-*, or *nat-*, then, implies some reference to *birth* or *being born*. Thus, a *native* of a locality was born there, one's *native* tongue is the one learned from early infancy; the *Nativity* is the birth of Christ.

Prenatal, then, must signify occurring *before birth*. Pregnant women in this country generally receive excellent *prenatal* care (that is, care *before the birth* of their infant); advances in *prenatal* diagnosis and treatment have sharply reduced the risks of childbearing, particularly for women over thirty.

Do you believe in *prenatal* influences? Do you think that a child while yet in its mother's womb will be affected by what happens to the parent? If the mother listens to symphonies and attends the opera while carrying the unborn child, will the infant grow up to be musically inclined? If she thinks only the most virtuous and noble of thoughts, will the infant show tendencies to become pure in heart and sterling in character? (Modern science scoffs at such *prenatal* influences, but this is a free country and you are privileged to hold any opinions you choose.)

DEFINITION

Prenatal means: previous to the birth of an infant.

PRONUNCIATION

Prenatal   pree-NAY′-təl

DERIVATION

Latin *prae*, before, and *natus*, be born.

47. RENASCENT

From another form of the Latin verb *be born*, namely *nasci*, comes *renascent*, *to be born again*. (*Re* generally signifies *back* or *again*, as in *repeat*, *revive*, *restore*, etc.) We may speak of the *renascent* economic power of Japan, meaning a *rebirth* of that power. The Second World War had destroyed much of the industrial base of the Japanese economy; in the years since the war, Japan has regained, and even surpassed, its prewar economic strength to become one of the leading industrial powers in the world.

Also, there has been a *renascence* of interest in an author who, not so long ago, was neglected, namely Henry James. Some of the styles in women's apparel represent a *renascence* of the fashion of earlier generations. *Renascence* always implies that something was once alive, eventually went into a state of neglect or figurative death, and was then revived. The word applies figuratively only to ideas, literary tastes, fashions, ways of thinking or acting, etc., never to actual death and rebirth of a living organism.

Another spelling of the same word is *renaissance*, with a different pronunciation, since this word, though still from the same Latin root *nasci*, came into English indirectly, through French.

When capitalized, *Renaissance* refers specifically to that rebirth of classical influence and learning that occurred in Europe in the fourteenth to sixteenth centuries.

DEFINITION

Renascent means: reborn; revived after a period of neglect.

PRONUNCIATIONS

Renascent	rə-NAS'-ənt
Renascence	rə-NAS'-əns
Renaissance	ren'-ə-SAHNS'

DERIVATION

Latin, *re*, again, plus *nasci*, be born.

48. INNATE

The prefix *in* may be negative in force, as in *inapplicable*, *not applicable*; or may mean *within*, as in *innate*.

Something, a quality, a characteristic, a defect, is *innate* if, in a sense, it was born within whatever possesses such quality, characteristic, or defect, rather than acquired from the outside. (Notice how clear cut the meaning of the word is when we can see the parts on which it is built; *in*, within, and *natus*, be born.)

When we speak of an *innate* quality of a living thing (the *innate* ferocity of the lion, a man's *innate* honesty, a woman's *innate* warmth, an athlete's *innate* strength and muscular coordination, etc.) we are implying that such a quality was, in a sense, present in the person or animal from birth, rather than acquired from the environment. Reading, for example, is not an *innate* ability, but thinking is.

When we talk, on the other hand, of an *innate* characteristic of nonliving matter (the *innate* defect of the plan, the *innate* weakness of the theory, the *innate* complexity of the mechanism, the *innate* tendency of a dictatorship to assume more and more power over the lives of the people), we refer to a characteristic that springs from the very nature and essence of the matter. The plan which has an *innate* defect could have no other, considering the type of plan it is; the *innate* weakness in the theory comes from the way the theory was evolved, etc. You see, then, the strong connection to birth or origin.

DEFINITION

Innate means: inborn, existing within; not acquired; so natural and deep seated as to seem to have been present since birth.

PRONUNCIATION

Innate   in-NAYT'

DERIVATION

Latin *in*, within, plus *natus*, be born.

49. PREMONITION

Moneo, monere, monitus is a Latin verb meaning *to warn*. The simple word *money* comes directly from this verb, in the following way. One of the ancient Roman goddesses was *Juno Moneta*, Juno the Warner, and it was in her temple that the coin of the realm was manufactured, on the theory that she would warn of approaching dangers, thieves, etc. *Monitor*, literally, is one who warns people to behave.

Examining *premonition*, then, we can see it as a warning (*monitus*) beforehand (*prae*); a foreboding. One may have a *premonition* of a coming disaster, a *premonition* of death, a *premonition* of failure. If a volcano gives a few *premonitory* rumbles, these are a warning of an eruption that may devastate the immediate region. You realize then, that a *premonition* is a feeling that something unpleasant, disastrous, or even catastrophic is about to occur. We do not, from the innate implication of the word, have *premonitions* of anything pleasant, happy, or delightful. People may have a *premonition*, or *premonitions*, of some untoward event, or certain phenomena themselves may be a *premonition* of that event. Disagreements between nations may be a *premonition* of war; a sudden drop in prices may be a *premonition* of hard times; rising unemployment may be a *premonition* of depression.

DEFINITION

Premonition means: a forewarning of coming disaster, a feeling of foreboding that an unpleasant event is about to occur.

PRONUNCIATIONS

Premonition   prem'-ə-NISH'-ən
Premonitory   prə-MON'-ə-tawr-ee

DERIVATION

Latin *prae*, before, plus *monitus*, to warn.

50. ADMONISH

Monitus, to warn, furnishes us with another valuable English word— *admonish*. A mother who *admonishes* her child combines a warning with a kindly, but serious, reproof. (For example, she might say, "Johnnie, I'd advise you to behave, or I'll be forced to punish you." This has all the attributes of an *admonition*—it's calm and gentle, but firm, and carries a warning of consequences.)

Reprove someone for a fault, but still maintain an air of friendly counseling, and you have another meaning of *admonish*. For example, "She repeatedly *admonished* her friend, but to no avail." The circumstances might have been as follows: Anna was in the habit of criticizing and quarreling with her husband Dick whenever they played canasta. Lois, Anna's friend, repeatedly advised that Dick's male ego was being hurt, and such advice was given out of a sincere desire to see that no untoward disaster befell the marriage. But Anna continued her criticism, and Dick finally ran off with his uncritical and adoring secretary.

To *admonish*, finally, may mean to caution against an act which the *admonisher* feels may have unfortunate results. Mothers *admonish* their daughters not to be too free with their affections; leaders during a war may *admonish* the people not to relax their efforts.

DEFINITION

Admonish means: (1) reprove kindly but firmly, with implications of warning; (2) reprove someone for a fault; (3) caution against an act.

PRONUNCIATIONS

Admonish	əd-MON′-ish
Admonition	ad-mə-NISH′-ən

DERIVATION

Latin *ad*, toward, plus *monitus*, warn.

Test Your Learning

I. TRUE OR FALSE?

1. *Prenatal* experiences can affect a child's life, according to latest scientific thinking. True False
2. There seems, in the past twenty years, to have been a *renascence* of Japanese industry. True False
3. Most people are *innately* vicious. True False
4. A *premonition* is a pleasant feeling. True False
5. People enjoy being *admonished*. True False

II. SAME OR OPPOSITE?

1. Prenatal—before birth Same Opposite
2. Renascent—reborn Same Opposite
3. Innate—acquired Same Opposite
4. Premonition—hindsight Same Opposite
5. Admonish—reprove Same Opposite

III. USE THE WORD

1. Her obstetrician gave her the best of _____ care.
2. He _____ his employee like a son.
3. Oak has a certain _____ strength that makes it excellent for use in furniture.
4. He sensed a _____ interest in long-neglected authors.
5. He had a _____ of his early death.

IV. WRITE THE WORD

1. Reprove gently 1. _____
2. Reborn 2. _____
3. Foreboding 3. _____
4. Before birth 4. _____
5. Inborn 5. _____

Check Your Learning

TEST I

  1—false, 2—true, 3—false, 4—false, 5—false.

TEST II

  1—same, 2—same, 3—opposite, 4—opposite, 5—same.

TEST III

  1—prenatal, 2—admonished, 3—innate, 4—renascent, 5—premonition.

TEST IV

  1—admonish, 2—renascent, 3—premonitory, 4—prenatal, 5—innate.

51. PRECLUDE

Prae, as we now know, is a Latin preposition which, when used as a prefix in English words, adds the meaning of "beforeness" to the root of the word. When so used as a prefix, *prae* is usually spelled *pre*.

There are countless examples of this function of *prae* (or *pre*). The Latin root *cedo* (spelled *cede* in English) means *to go*. *Secede* is *to go away*, or withdraw; *accede* is *to go toward*, or agree; and *precede* is *to go before*. We are already familiar with *prenatal*, before birth, and *premonition*, a warning beforehand. *Premeditate* is *to plan beforehand; predict* is *to say beforehand*, or foretell; *prejudice* is *to judge beforehand*; and there are such self-explanatory terms as *precook, predestined, predate, precancel*.

Let us now see what happens when the Latin verb *claudere*, to close or shut, is combined with the prefix *pre*.

Claudere is usually spelled *-clude* in English. It is found in such common words as *include*, literally close in; *conclude*, literally close (something) together, bring to an end, or come to the end of a reasoning process; *seclude*, shut away by itself; *exclude*, shut out.

If we combine the Latin verb *claudere* with the preposition *prae*, we get (in the English spelling) *preclude*, which, by an analysis of its parts, means *shut beforehand*.

Let us examine how the literal meanings of the parts of *preclude* build up into the general and extended significance which this useful English verb now has.

I may say to you: "I shall explain this process so completely and clearly as to *preclude* any confusion." What I am doing is shutting off confusion *before* it starts.

Or I may say that if we guard the prisoner day and night, we will *preclude* any possibility of his committing suicide. What are we doing? We are shutting out the possibility *before* it happens.

Or I may say that the senator resigned his office in order, his opponents thought, to *preclude* a congressional investigation of his campaign expenditures. Again, one act prevents, *beforehand*, the occurrence of another—shuts it out from the possibility of occurrence.

Or, finally, I may say: "John's marrying this girl does not *preclude* my seeing her if I wish to." John's act, in short, does not shut out, *before* it happens, an act that I may be contemplating.

Preclude, then, stresses that certain acts or circumstances or measures effectively shut out the possibility of an occurrence.

DEFINITION

Preclude means: to prevent the presence, existence, or occurrence of something; make impossible; prevent a person from doing something; forestall.

PRONUNCIATION

Preclude   prə-KLOOD' (Last syllable rhymes with *mood*).

DERIVATION

Prae, before, plus *claudere*, to shut.

USAGE CAUTION

An act, circumstance, etc., may *preclude* some other act; or may *preclude* a person from doing something, as in "We will take measures to *preclude* any escape," or "We will take measures to *preclude* him *from* escaping."

52. RECLUSE

Latin verbs, as you know, may have a number of variant forms, and English words may be built on one or more of these forms. We have already seen that linguistic process at work in the verb *nasci, natus*, the first form of which gives us *renascent*, the second *prenatal, innate*, etc.

The Latin verb *to shut* has two forms, *claudere* and *clausus*, and our new word *recluse* is built on the second form.

The *recluse* is a person who has voluntarily shut himself away from the world, perhaps for religious reasons, perhaps from such personal causes as sorrow over a loved one's death, deep disappointment or frustration in a love affair, or general inability to get along with people.

It takes, of course, a special kind of personality to become a *recluse*. To shut oneself off from all intercourse with people, whatever the surface motivation, implies deep and perhaps unconscious hostility to the world. The *recluse* may seem to be the gentlest and kindest of persons, and often is, consciously. But you can bet something happened way back in this person's life to build up a distrust in other people, an inability to get comfort and satisfaction from fellow humans.

Then comes some external circumstance such as a death, a disappointment, a strong rebuke, or sometimes even something comparatively trivial, and all the unconscious forces suddenly explode. Result: the potential *recluse* resigns from the human race, signifying that he no longer feels capable of handling personal relations with other people.

DEFINITION

A *recluse* is one who voluntarily leads a solitary life, secludes himself from the world, shuts himself away from human intercourse.

PRONUNCIATION

Recluse   REK′-lo͞os *or* rə-KLO͞OS′ (Last syllable rhymes with *juice*).

DERIVATION

Re, back, plus *claudere, clausus*, to shut

53. CLAUSTROPHOBIA

The Latin verb *to close, claudere, clausus*, is the origin of another fascinating English word, *claustrophobia*, which is the term that describes a psychological and morbid dread of confined spaces, crowds, small rooms, and other closed-in places.

The word has been used very loosely, loose usage being a fate which overtakes any scientific term that enters the general vocabulary. "That place is enough to give me *claustrophobia*!" exclaims your friend, most inaccurately but very descriptively. For a true *claustrophobe* has not contracted his mental ailment from exposure to confining places, but from some early emotional experiences which cause him to react as he does to lack of room. What these experiences were may vary considerably with the individual, but the symptoms are fairly typical. The victim of *claustrophobia* is unable, psychologically, to enter any narrow passages or any shut-in or closely walled-in spaces, almost as if someone or something were holding him back physically; or if he finds himself by accident in such a place, hemmed in by people or walls, he has an overwhelming compulsion, a morbid and irresistible need, to escape. *Claustrophobes* are, of course, emotionally unstable, and *claustrophobia* is just one of the ways their instability, anxiety, or maladjustment is manifested.

DEFINITION

Claustrophobia is the medical and psychiatric term for the morbid dread of constricting areas, crowds, and confining places.

PRONUNCIATIONS

Claustrophobia	klaw'-strə-FŌ'-bee-ə
Claustrophobe	KLAW'-strə-fōb'
Claustrophobic	klaw'-strə-FŌ'-bik

DERIVATION

From Latin *clausus*, close, plus Greek *phobia*, morbid dread.

54. AGORAPHOBIA

The opposite mental ailment to *claustrophobia* is *agoraphobia*, which is formed on two Greek roots, *agora*, the market place, and *phobia*, morbid dread. The *agoraphobe*, again an individual of unstable emotions, has symptoms of morbid anxiety and violent, baseless fear in relation to wide or open spaces. The person of *agoraphobic* tendencies will dread crossing a wide parkway, would rather die than find himself in a large, empty ballroom, an expanse of beach or lawn, or any similarly unconstricted place. This ailment is no less common than *claustrophobia*, but the term to describe it is less familiar to most people.

DEFINITION

Agoraphobia is the medical and psychiatric term for that emotional block which causes great fear and anxiety in wide or open spaces.

PRONUNCIATIONS

Agoraphobia	ag'-ə-rə-FŌ'-bee-ə
Agoraphobe	AG'-ə-rə-fōb'
Agoraphobic	ag'-ə-rə-FŌ'-bik

From Greek *agora*, market place (in Ancient Greece the market place was in the open) plus *phobia*, morbid dread.

55. ACROPHOBIA

The least known, but no less common, of the three standard phobias is *acrophobia*, which combines the root *phobia* with *acros*, highest. (*Acros* is also found in the everyday word *acrobat*, strictly one who goes on tiptoe or climbs up high.) The *acrophobe* has the same morbid dread of heights that the *claustrophobe* feels for confinement and the *agoraphobe* for open spaces. We all experience a touch of fear when we climb a high pole or ladder or look down from the roof of a skyscraper—but the *acrophobe* is absolutely petrified. Since *acrophobia* is a deep-seated psychological malady, no element of logic or realistic values enters into the *acrophobe*'s fear—he can be 100% safe from falling, and can realize his complete safety intellectually, but his emotional reactions are beyond his control. Result: He can never permit himself to climb beyond a certain distance, or, if he should find himself at any height, safe or not, he simply goes to pieces. Obviously, victims of *acrophobia* and people with *acrophobic* tendencies never ride in airplanes or elevators, climb beyond the first three steps of a ladder, nor become professional tightrope walkers.

DEFINITION

Acrophobia is the medical and psychiatric term for a morbid dread of heights.

PRONUNCIATIONS

Acrophobia	ak'-rə-FŌ'-bee-ə
Acrophobe	AK'-rə-fōb'
Acrophobic	ak'-rə-FŌ'-bik

DERIVATION

Greek *acros*, highest place, plus *phobia*, morbid dread.

A NOTE ON PHOBIAS

The general word *phobia*, like the specific terms *claustrophobia*, *agoraphobia*, and *acrophobia*, has become part of the layman's vocabulary and has a much looser everyday meaning than it does in medical and psychiatric parlance.

Psychiatrically, a phobia is a dread so deep-seated, so strong, and so unreasonable that it impairs the efficiency of the individual who is a victim of it; but in general usage the term has come to mean simply an unreasonable fear of, or even a great aversion to something. You may hear a parent say that her child has a *phobia* for the dark, meaning no more, perhaps, than that the youngster is uncomfortable and unhappy unless a light is left on at bedtime. Since words alter in meaning according to common acceptance, such usage of *phobia* is *not* incorrect; it is simply an extension of the original, and technical or medical, sense of the word.

Psychiatry recognizes scores of true phobias. *Claustro-, agora-,* and *acrophobia* are the three that have come into general use, but there are also, among many others, *nyctophobia* (fear of darkness), *pyrophobia* (fear of fire), *ailurophobia* (fear of cats), *triskaidekaphobia* (fear of the "unlucky" numeral 13), etc. *Hydrophobia*, which breaks down etymologically into fear of water, is, in actuality, the popular term for *rabies*, a fatal and infectious disease of mammals. The term *hydrophobia* was attached to the ailment because of the difficulty of swallowing water in animals afflicted with it. It is not, however, a morbid dread of water.

Test Your Learning

I. TRUE OR FALSE?

1. If one action *precludes* another, it rules out the possibility of its occurrence.	True False
2. A *recluse* enjoys group activities.	True False
3. *Claustrophobia* is morbid dread of crowds and confined places.	True False
4. *Agoraphobia* is fear of heights.	True False
5. *Acrophobia* is a fear of open spaces.	True False

II. SAME OR OPPOSITE?

1. Preclude—rule out	Same Opposite
2. Recluse—hermit	Same Opposite
3. Claustrophobia—agoraphobia	Same Opposite
4. Acrophobia—fear of heights	Same Opposite
5. Agoraphobia—fear of closed spaces	Same Opposite

III. USE THE WORD

1. A victim of severe _____, he refused to visit anyone who lived above the second story of an apartment house.
2. He felt most uncomfortable in small rooms and wondered if he suffered from _____.
3. Inhabitants of the Wide West had better not be _____.
4. After the death of his wife, he found it impossible to live in the company of men; he became a _____.
5. Aggressive action now may _____ attack by the enemy later.

IV. WRITE THE WORD

1. A hermit—someone who lives in seclusion   1. _____
2. Fear of wide spaces   2. _____
3. Forestall   3. _____
4. Fear of heights   4. _____
5. Fear of closed places   5. _____

Check Your Learning

ANSWERS TO TESTS ON UNIT 10

TEST I

1—true, 2—false, 3—true, 4—false, 5—false.

TEST II

1—same, 2—same, 3—opposite, 4—same, 5—opposite.

TEST III

1—acrophobia, 2—claustrophobia, 3—agoraphobes, 4—recluse, 5—preclude.

TEST IV

1—recluse, 2—agoraphobia, 3—preclude, 4—acrophobia, 5—claustrophobia.

Unit Eleven

56. CUPIDITY

Cupid, as you know, is the god of love, according to ancient Roman mythology, and is today generally represented, pictorially, as a naked young boy with wings. He usually has with him his chief weapon, a bow and arrow, and anyone he shoots, so goes the fable, falls in love on sight with the first person he (or, of course, she) meets. I guess this is as reasonable an explanation as any of why people fall in love, though psychiatry maintains that the prime cause is that the object of one's affection fulfills some unconscious need. In any case, the name Cupid comes from the Latin noun *cupiditas*, desire, and it is this noun which is the direct origin of the English word *cupidity*. *Cupidity*, too, is desire, but of a very different sort from that with which Cupid's arrows supposedly infect people. The desire associated with *cupidity* is for the possession not of a loved one, but of material wealth. Such desire is intense, compelling, greedy, and altogether insatiable—if we speak of a man's *cupidity*, we mean that no matter how much he has he wants more. After his first million, he goes after the second—and with the same neurotic intensity. *Cupidity* is such uncontrolled need for possessions that it passes all bounds of reasons—talk of a person's *cupidity* and you imply that he covets and lusts after more money, houses, real estate, factories, oil lands, buildings, automobiles, yachts, etc., than he can possibly use in a dozen lifetimes.

Nations as well as people can be afflicted with *cupidity*—then the desire is for conquest of more and more and more territory. And in the case of nations, as in men, such inordinate desire springs from deep feelings of inadequacy; they can prove their worth, so they feel, only by what they own. But of course if they possessed the entire world (and often they come close to it), they would still be riddled with gnawing doubts of their adequacy, and so they would have to push on for further material gains.

So those unhappy mortals who, by word or action, seem to say, "See my expensive new car (or my beautiful mink coat)—don't you envy me?" really mean, whether they realize it or not, "All these possessions

I have acquired should prove to you that I'm as good as you are—though deep down I wish I could convince myself also."

DEFINITION

Cupidity means: inordinate, insatiable desire for wealth or possessions.

PRONUNCIATION

Cupidity   kyoo-PID′-ə-tee
  (There is no adjective form of this noun.)

DERIVATION

From Latin *cupiditas*, desire.

27. CONCUPISCENCE

The passionate desire for wealth connoted by *cupidity* is, perhaps, say the psychiatrists, a compensation for inhibited, frustrated, or inadequate desires of another sort. The Latin noun *cupiditas* is derived from the verb *cupio*, to desire, and it is on one of the forms of this verb that the English word *concupiscence* is built. *Concupiscence* is inordinate and intemperate desire for sexual gratification, and the person you label *concupiscent* is, in your mind, lustful, unduly sensual, constantly longing to satisfy his physical appetites.

  Concupiscent is, of course, an emotionally charged and judgmental word. Call someone *concupiscent* and you say much more than that, in your opinion, his sexual appetites are strong; you are also rendering the judgment that such a person acts and feels in a way you do not condone and for which you personally have only contempt.

DEFINITION

Concupiscence means: intemperate desire, lust, sexual longing.

PRONUNCIATIONS

Concupiscence   kən-KYOO-pə-səns
Concupiscent   kən-KYOO-pə-sənt

DERIVATION

From Latin *cupio*, to desire.

58. IMPEDE

When we speak of parts of the body, we may do so either literally or figuratively. Literally, the mouth is the organ of absorption of food, the stomach the organ of digestion. Figuratively, when you call a person "a big mouth," you mean that he talks too much and when, again figuratively, you claim you cannot "stomach" so much talk you mean that you dislike, or cannot tolerate, it.

Foot, too, can be used figuratively. Literally, an infant may put "his foot in his mouth," but when we say that every time a person "opens his mouth he puts his foot into it," we communicate an entirely different thought with the same expression. If, figuratively, you put your foot in the way of someone's activity, you hinder him, slow down his progress, or get in his way.

The Latin root for *foot* is *pedis*, found in such common English words as *pedestrian*, one who walks on foot; *pedal*, pertaining to the foot, or a lever worked by the foot, as in a bicycle; *pedestal*, a platform on which a person or statue stands (on foot). The same root is found in *impede*, which etymologically means to *entangle the feet*, and may be used both literally and figuratively, though it is most commonly employed in the figurative sense.

Literally, anyone's progress in walking or moving is *impeded* if his feet become entangled in ropes, chains, etc.; stiff shoes may *impede* one's movement by actually making walking more difficult; or deep mud can *impede* motion by holding back, or slowing down, the feet.

Figuratively, to *impede* means to make progress very difficult, to slow down an action or activity, to impose upon a person or action such obstacles as to make progress or success difficult. *Impede* someone and you make life hard for him, but you do not stop him completely; you merely get in his way, or put obstacles in his way. Now the progress, action, or activity that is *impeded* need not be actual motion. We may say, for example, that the normal development of children is often *impeded* by their parents' old-fashioned notions—notice that the development doesn't stop, but is only made difficult or slowed down.

Or we may say that the young instructor's teaching was constantly *impeded* by the undisciplined behavior of his students. Again, teaching was not made impossible by such student reactions, but nearly so.

Anything which *impedes* is an *impediment*. A speech *impediment*, for example, makes talking slow or difficult or awkward, but does not necessarily silence the speaker. And a person, too, can be an *impediment*, as the husband who is an *impediment* to a wife's illicit plans, or as a wife who insults her husband's business associates and is thereby an *impediment* to his business success.

DEFINITION

Impede means: to get in the way of, literally or figuratively, and thus make an activity more difficult.

PRONUNCIATIONS

Impede	im-PEED′
Impediment	im-PED′-ə-mənt

DERIVATION

Latin *pedis*, foot.

59. EXPEDITE

You can use your foot, then, to get in someone's way, and thus slow him up—you can also use it to kick him forward more quickly. Or, if we analyze it from the other point of view, if your feet are entangled, progress is difficult—if your feet are freed from all possible entanglements, you can speed ahead.

Ex is a Latin preposition which means *out* (an *exit*, for example, is a door that leads *out*, an *exile* is one who has been put *out* of a country, etc.). Combine *ex* as a prefix with *pedis*, foot, and, etymologically,* you take one's feet *out* of the entanglement; in short, you *expedite* results, an activity, the movement of something, someone's progress, etc.

To *expedite*, then, is to speed up progress, contrasted with *impede*, which is to slow it down; and this speeding up is made possible by removing obstacles or impediments, by figuring out quicker or simpler means, by using more efficient methods, not just by going faster. In any large industrial plant, for example, there is generally an *expediter*—a man whose job it is to see that production is carried on efficiently and therefore speedily, who guards against that type of wasteful and bungling activity that would slow up production or packing or shipping.

The adjective form of *expedite* is *expeditious*. *Expeditious* means to an end are those that accomplish the end most quickly because most ef-

*This word as used throughout the book means *by derivation; etymology* is the study of roots and word origins.

82

ficiently; an *expeditious* way of doing something is the best and fastest; and to accomplish something *expeditiously* is to lose no time in bungling or waste motion.

To *expedite* a delivery, similarly, is to see that it is sent on its way as soon as possible; to *expedite* the movement of troops is to remove all factors that might hold them back.

DEFINITION

Expedite means: to accelerate progress by removing all bars to speed and efficiency; to speed up, but always in conjunction with the removal of delaying or complicating obstacles.

PRONUNCIATIONS

Expedite	EKS-pə-dīt′
Expeditious	eks′-pə-DISH′-əs
Expeditiously	eks′-pə-DISH′-əs-lee

DERIVATION

From *ex*, out, plus *pedis*, foot.

60. PEDESTRIAN

Pedis is the Latin root for *foot*, we now know, and a *pedestrian*, of course, covers distances on foot. To go from here to there on foot may be healthful and relaxing—but it is by no means as rapid nor as imaginative as using a bicycle, horse, motor car, train, or airplane.

Pedestrian used as a noun (i.e., one who walks) is too simple a word to merit further consideration—but *pedestrian* is also used as an adjective, in phrases like "a *pedestrian* style of writing," "a *pedestrian* approach to life," "a *pedestrian* way of doing things," etc. In such instances the word has undergone a kind of poetic or figurative extension of meaning, and signifies slow, plodding, halting, commonplace, and unimaginative—not any one of these descriptives, but a combination of all of them. To accuse an author of *pedestrianism* is one of the most devastating criticisms to make; to say that a man is *pedestrian* in his attitudes is equally insulting, since the implication is that he is heavyhanded, slow-witted, unimaginative, etc. The use of the word *pedestrian* implies, in fine, that the person it applies to walks when we would expect him to ride or fly.

DEFINITION

Pedestrian (adj.) means: slow, plodding, commonplace, and unimaginative.

PRONUNCIATIONS

Pedestrian	pə-DES′-tree-ən
Pedestrianism	pə-DES′-tree-ən-iz-əm

DERIVATION

Latin *pedis*, foot.

Test Your Learning

I. TRUE OR FALSE?

1. *Cupidity* shows a well-adjusted personality.　　　　　　True　False
2. *Concupiscence* is held in high esteem in this country.　True　False
3. An *impeding* factor slows down the progress of something.　　　　　　True　False
4. To *expedite* matters is to speed them up.　　　　　　True　False
5. The author who possesses a *pedestrian* style shows that he has a fertile imagination and a lively gift for writing.　True　False

II. SAME OR OPPOSITE?

1. Cupidity—generosity　　　　　Same　Opposite
2. Concupiscent—sexless　　　　Same　Opposite
3. Impede—provide obstacles　　Same　Opposite
4. Expedite—Slow down　　　　Same　Opposite
5. Pedestrian (adj.)—original　　Same　Opposite

III. USE THE WORD

1. The _____ plot of his new novel is a great disappointment to his public.
2. His lack of audacity has always served to _____ his success.
3. You will _____ matters greatly if you get your reports in a few days earlier than usual.
4. He strikes us as being a most lustful and _____ character.
5. A child who is brought up in dire poverty by parents who are openly contemptuous of him is likely to show strong tendencies toward _____ when he grows up.

IV. WRITE THE WORD

1. Inordinate desire for material wealth
2. To present obstacles
3. To hasten
4. Sexual longing
5. Unimaginative, slow, etc.

1. _____
2. _____
3. _____
4. _____
5. _____

Check Your Learning

ANSWERS TO TESTS ON UNIT 11

TEST I

1—false, 2—false, 3—true, 4—true, 5—false.

TEST II

1—opposite, 2—opposite, 3—same, 4—opposite, 5—opposite.

TEST III

1—pedestrian, 2—impede, 3—expedite, 4—concupiscent, 5—cupidity.

TEST IV

1—cupidity, 2—impede, 3—expedite, 4—concupiscence, 5—pedestrian.

Unit Twelve

61. ADHERENT

In Latin, *haerere* is a verb meaning *to stick*, in the sense that glue sticks to paper. Another form of this verb is *haesitus*, a form on which are built the terms *adhesive* (as in *adhesive* tape) and *adhesion* (a medical word signifying the sticking together of internal tissues which are normally separated). *Adhesions* often occur after an operation, and are, so say the victims, excruciatingly painful, hence an integral part of the type of conversation which starts with "Have you heard about my operation?"

Adherent, the word under present discussion, obviously also has about it a sense of *sticking to* (*ad* is a prefix meaning *to* or *toward*), but the sticking is figurative rather than literal. An *adherent* of the Roman Catholic church is one who is mentally, emotionally, or morally attached to that religion; in other words a follower of the church and its principles. One can also be an *adherent* of the Republican party, of the Henry George school of economic thinking (Single Tax); of the philosophy of free trade; of the welfare state; or of the theory that pain is superior to pleasure. In short, one can be an *adherent* of any principle of thinking—religious, moral, economic, political, social. Or one can *adhere* or show *adherence* to such doctrines of thought or action.

DEFINITION

Adherent means: a follower of some doctrine of thought or action.

PRONUNCIATIONS

Adherent   ad-HEER′-ənt
Adhere   ad-HEER′
Adherence ad-HEER′-əns

DERIVATION

From Latin *haero*, to stick, plus *ad*, to.

62. INCOHERENT

Haero, then, is *to stick*, and *con* is a Latin preposition meaning *together*. *Con* is also spelled, in English words, *co, col, cor, com*, etc. (*collaborate*, work together, *cooperate*, operate together, *compatible*, feeling together or harmonious, *concoct*, cook together, and many others). *Coherence*, then, is a *sticking together*, and refers to a unity of immaterial or intangible qualities, such as the content of speech or writing, the plot or details of a novel, the points of an argument, etc. As it happens, the negative form of the word, namely *incoherent*, is the more frequently used. When we say that someone spoke *incoherently*, we mean that the content of his communication was rambling, disjointed, unconnected, showing no logical thinking, in fine *not sticking together* logically or sensibly.

A person may become *incoherent* with rage, fear, or ecstasy—it will then be difficult or impossible to see any continuity or rational sequence in what he is saying, for he will leave sentences half-finished, flit from thought to thought and point to point.

If the parts of an essay, or musical composition, or work of art, do not *cohere*, again a logical or understandable organization is missing. Some readers find the writings of Gertrude Stein, James Joyce, and Ezra Pound largely *incoherent*, though the devotees of these authors claim that it is the rest of the world, not they, who are crazy.

DEFINITION

Incoherent means: without logical connection, so rambling as to defy comprehension, not sticking together logically or sensibly.

PRONUNCIATIONS

Incoherent	in'-kō-HEER'-ənt
Coherent	kō-HEER'-ənt
Incoherence	in'-kō-HEER'-əns
Coherence	kō-HEER'-əns
Cohere	kō-HEER'

DERIVATION

Latin *haero*, to stick, plus *con*, together.

63. INHERENT

Is evil an *inherent* part of man's nature? Or are human beings *inherently* good? This is the type of philosophical discussion that can go on for hours or days before any conclusion is reached, and probably both questions are so phrased as to be unanswerable, "good" and "evil" being such vague and relative terms.

An *inherent* quality of a person or thing is a permanent and inseparable element—it is permanently *stuck within* that person or thing. *In*, you will discover as you continue to study the root structure of words, is a prefix that may serve in three different ways. It may function to make a word *negative* (compatible, *in*compatible; coherent, *in*coherent; comprehensible, *in*comprehensible). It may mean *in* or *within* (*in*herent, *in*nate, *in*coming, *in*grained). Or it may intensify the meaning of the root (*in*valuable, *in*flammable).

Inherent, then, is synonymous with *innate*, the word we studied in Unit 9; the distinction between the words is not in meaning or use, but only in derivation. *Innate* by origin means *born within* and therefore essential, basic, rather than acquired; *inherent* by origin signifies *stuck within* and therefore essential, inseparable, basic.

If we say that justice *inheres* in a democratic state, we mean that the quality is inseparable from democracy, that the two inseparably are stuck together. Thus also, sympathy may be *inherent* in a certain family, hardness is *inherent* in diamonds, fatalism is an *inherent* part of the Arab's religion, humbleness is *inherent* in all religions.

Innate generally applies to living creatures, since it refers to birth; *inherent* may apply to institutions, ideas, plans, theories, etc., as well as to animate forms.

DEFINITION

Inherent means: existing in something as a permanent and inseparable quality.

PRONUNCIATIONS

Inherent	in-HEER'-ənt
Inhere	in-HEER'

DERIVATION

From Latin *haero*, stick, and *in*, within.

64. FORTE

The Latin adjective *fortis*, strong, is found in such common words as *fort* or *fortress*, a strong place, protected from military attack; and *fortify*, make stronger, either in a military sense (*fortify* the city) or in other respects (*fortify* himself with liquor before the interview, *fortify* his position by buying out his competitor, *fortified* by a belief in God, etc.). The root is also found in *forte*, one's strong point, an area of living in which one excels by virtue of skill or knowledge.

In a social gathering, for example, the conversation may turn to the relative worth of two competing baseball teams, and a controversy may arise as to whether team A has better pitchers than team B. "Let's hear Jim's opinion," someone may say. "He knows all about baseball. In fact, it's his *forte*." Now bear in mind that Jim need not be connected professionally with baseball, baseball may not be his business, but he has built up a strong knowledge of the game and its players.

Description of characters in emotional turmoil may be the *forte* of one author, an aspect of life he is exceptionally expert at portraying, while tender love scenes may be the *forte* of another. A certain painter may excel in seascapes, another in portraits—each, again, has a particular *forte*. Cooking may be the *forte* of Mrs. A and the rearing of happy children may be Mrs. B's *forte*.

DEFINITION

Forte means: one's strong point.

PRONUNCIATION

Forte   FAWRT

(The two-syllable pronunciation of this word [FOR-tay] is considered uncultivated and unacceptable.)

DERIVATION

Latin *fortis*, strong.

65. FORTITUDE

Strength, then, may come from military impregnability (*fort*, *fortress*, *fortify*), from a unique expertness in a particular area of living (*forte*), or, as in the case of *fortitude*, which also derives from the Latin adjective *fortis*, from emotional resources.

Fortitude is a kind of bravery, but not the kind that sends men into battle, firemen up high ladders and into blazing buildings, or bachelors into ill-considered marriages. Rather, *fortitude* is emotional strength to endure suffering and hardship without complaint; it is a kind of moral courage to keep on patiently and firmly when things look bleakest, when privation is at its worst, when continued resistance seems most futile. *Fortitude* is a combination, you might say, of grit, pluck, guts, and sand.

In the early days of World War II, when the allies were experiencing dark days, Fiorello La Guardia, the peppy and stalwart little mayor of New York City, used to start his weekly radio broadcast with the phrase "Patience and Fortitude," both of which qualities were most needful at that time. The person who can live in poverty or illness without complaining, who can accept the blows of fate without flinching, who has a great degree of emotional resiliency and moral fiber, so that misfortunes and disasters do not terrify him—such a person can be said to possess *fortitude*. And it is, strangely, a quality that few people realize they have until they really need it. It is a quiet, unspectacular sort of courage.

DEFINITION

Fortitude means: patient courage under affliction; moral strength and
    endurance under adverse circumstances.

PRONUNCIATION

Fortitude   FAWR-tə-tōōd

DERIVATION

From Latin *fortis*, strong.

Test Your Learning

I. TRUE OR FALSE?

1. An *adherent* of Sigmund Freud is a believer in psycho-
   analysis.   *True*   *False*
2. Rage may make a normally eloquent speaker *incoherent*.   *True*   *False*
3. A company with the *inherent* strength of a mountain is
   in a good financial position.   *True*   *False*
4. *Forte* refers to a skill which is being newly learned.   *True*   *False*
5. A person of *fortitude* usually breaks under adversity.   *True*   *False*

II. SAME OR OPPOSITE?

1. Adherent—follower
2. Incoherent—logical
3. Inherent—innate
4. Forte—talent
5. Fortitude—cowardice

Same   Opposite
Same   Opposite
Same   Opposite
Same   Opposite
Same   Opposite

III. USE THE WORD

1. If he did not possess almost superhuman _____, he could never have come through his wife's agonizing illness so well.
2. Canasta is his _____, so it is not surprising that he brought his team to victory.
3. His _____ to the old-fashioned virtues of honesty and tolerance is most refreshing.
4. He spoke so _____ about his experiences that it was easy to realize what a devastating effect they had on him.
5. There is, say some philosophers, a (an) _____ amount of good in the worst of us.

IV. THINK OF THE WORD

1. Special talent; strong point
2. Follower; believer
3. Integral, inseparable
4. Patient courage
5. Rambling; incomprehensible

1. _____
2. _____
3. _____
4. _____
5. _____

Check Your Learning

ANSWERS TO TESTS ON UNIT 12

TEST I

1—true, 2—true, 3—true, 4—false, 5—false.

TEST II

1—same, 2—opposite, 3—same, 4—same, 5—opposite.

TEST III

1—fortitude, 2—forte, 3—adherence, 4—incoherently, 5—inherent.

TEST IV

1—forte, 2—adherent, 3—inherent, 4—fortitude, 5—incoherent.

Review Test III

(A Complete Check on Your Understanding of Words 46–65)

A. SAME OR OPPOSITE?

	Same	Opposite
1. prenatal—before birth	Same	Opposite
2. renascent—reborn	Same	Opposite
3. innate—inherent	Same	Opposite
4. premonition—foreboding	Same	Opposite
5. admonish—caution	Same	Opposite
6. preclude—make possible	Same	Opposite
7. recluse—hermit	Same	Opposite
8. claustrophobia—fear of open spaces	Same	Opposite
9. agoraphobia—fear of closed spaces	Same	Opposite
10. acrophobia—fear of heights	Same	Opposite
11. cupidity—greed	Same	Opposite
12. concupiscent—ascetic	Same	Opposite
13. impede—help	Same	Opposite
14. expedite—slow down	Same	Opposite
15. pedestrian—lively	Same	Opposite
16. adherent—follower	Same	Opposite
17. incoherent—clear	Same	Opposite
18. inherent—inseparable	Same	Opposite
19. forte—excellence	Same	Opposite
20. fortitude—courage	Same	Opposite

B. USE THE WORD (1)

From Column I, choose the word which most effectively completes the pattern of each phrase in Column II.

I	II
1. claustrophobe	a—_____ influences
2. admonish	b—_____ interest in virtue
3. agoraphobe	c—_____ strength
4. innate	d—_____ of disaster
5. prenatal	e—_____ him to behave
6. recluse	f—_____ his being accepted by vilifying his character
7. acrophobe	g—became a _____ after the death of his wife
8. preclude	h—a (an) _____ dislikes crowds
9. renascent	i—a (an) _____ hates open space
10. premonition	j—a (an) _____ fears heights

C. USE THE WORD (2)

Follow directions for Test B.

I	II
1. cupidity	a— _____ their retreat and save them from capture
2. concupiscent	
3. impeding	b—a (an) _____ of communism
4. expedite	c—his insatiable _____
5. pedestrian (adj.)	d—_____ virtue
6. adherent	e—his _____ and, in fact, his greatest interest
7. incoherent	
8. inherent	f—angered him by _____ his progress
9. forte	
10. fortitude	g—in admiration of his patience and _____
	h—a (an) _____ leer
	i—_____ with rage
	j—a (an) _____ style of writing

D. FIND THE MEANING (1)

From Column II, find the word that best fits each meaning in Column I.

I	II
1. rebirth	a—prenatal
2. prior to being born	b—premonitory
3. inborn	c—recluse
4. forewarning	d—agoraphobic
5. make impossible	e—cupidity
6. one who has withdrawn from the world	f—acrophobic
7. shunning narrow places	g—renascence
8. shunning open places	h—preclude
9. shunning high places	i—claustrophobic
10. greed	j—innate

E. FIND THE MEANING (2)

Follow directions for Test D.

I	II
1. firm but gentle rebuke	a—adherence
2. sexual longing	b—expedite
3. bar	c—inherent
4. hasten	d—forte

93

5. unimaginative
6. attachment
7. logically organized
8. integral and inseparable
9. strong point
10. moral courage and strength

e—admonition
f—coherent
g—impediment
h—pedestrian
i—concupiscence
j—fortitude

F. THINK OF THE WORD

Write the word that suits each brief definition. As a complete test of your learning, do *not* refer to previous lists of the required words.

1. Rebuke firmly but in a friendly fashion   1. _____
2. Hasten by removing bars to speed and efficiency   2. _____
3. Integral and inseparable   3. _____
4. Fear of heights   4. _____
5. Fear of open places   5. _____
6. Fear of confined spaces   6. _____
7. One who prefers permanent seclusion   7. _____
8. Before birth   8. _____
9. Moral or emotional strength and patient endurance   9. _____
10. Make impossible   10. _____
11. Inordinate desire for wealth, territory, or material possessions   11. _____
12. Born again   12. _____
13. Unoriginal, slow, halting   13. _____
14. Get in the way of   14. _____
15. Inborn; not acquired   15. _____
16. A prewarning   16. _____
17. Sexually desirous   17. _____
18. A follower of or believer in   18. _____
19. One's strong point   19. _____
20. Rambling, unconnected   20. _____

Check Your Learning

ANSWERS TO REVIEW TEST III

A

1—same, 2—same, 3—same, 4—same, 5—same, 6—opposite, 7—same, 8—opposite, 9—opposite, 10—same, 11—same, 12—opposite, 13—opposite, 14—opposite, 15—opposite, 16—same, 17—opposite, 18—same, 19—same, 20—same.

B

1—h, 2—e, 3—i, 4—c, 5—a, 6—g, 7—j, 8—f, 9—b, 10—d.

C

1—c, 2—h, 3—f, 4—a, 5—j, 6—b, 7—i, 8—d, 9—e, 10—g.

D

1—g, 2—a, 3—j, 4—b, 5—h, 6—c, 7—i, 8—d, 9—f, 10—e.

E

1—e, 2—i, 3—g, 4—b, 5—h, 6—a, 7—f, 8—c, 9—d, 10—j.

F

1—admonish, 2—expedite, 3—inherent, 4—acrophobia, 5—agoraphobia, 6—claustrophobia, 7—recluse, 8—prenatal, 9—fortitude, 10—preclude, 11—cupidity, 12—renascent, 13—pedestrian, 14—impede, 15—innate, 16—premonition, 17—concupiscent, 18—adherent, 19—forte, 20—incoherent.

PART IV

Types

The twenty words in the next four units will deal with various types of humanity. How many of these questions can you correctly answer?

1. What does an *atheist* not believe in?
2. In what areas is a *connoisseur*'s judgment valuable?
3. What is the forte of the *lothario*?
4. What are the hobbies of the *philatelist*, the *numismatist*, the *bibliophile*, the *balletomane*, and the *antiquarian*?
5. What's wrong with the *sadist*, the *masochist*, the *charlatan*?
6. What is the chief interest of the *thespian*, of the *terpsichorean*?
7. Where would you be likely to find a *naiad*, a *nimrod*?

Do you really understand these words?
Could you use them successfully, effectively?
Read on . . .

Unit Thirteen

It takes all kinds to make a world, says the old, threadbare adage, but trite as the thought is, it is nevertheless true.

We are going to examine, in Part IV, a few of the many types of people there are in the world; we are going to discuss the way they think and act and feel.

66. ATHEIST

The greatest bulk of humanity, as far back as recorded history goes and probably even in prehistoric times, has believed in and worshiped a supernatural or supreme force which has been accepted as controlling and shaping the world. The ancient Greeks and Romans had a number of gods, each presiding over a limited area of life. The ancient Hebrews introduced to civilization the concept of a single, all-powerful, all-present, all-knowing deity, and the present Christian and Jewish religions likewise accept but one God.

Paralleling the general acceptance through history of a deity or deities, there has also been the minority, nonconformist opinion, to wit: there is no God, in man's image or otherwise. The adherents of this philosophy, those who definitely deny the existence of a supreme being, are known as *atheists*.

DEFINITION

Atheist: one who rejects the concept of a supreme deity.

PRONUNCIATIONS

Atheist	AY'-thee-ist
Atheism	AY'-thee-iz-əm
Atheistic	ay'-thee-IS'-tik

DERIVATION

Greek *theos*, God, plus the negative prefix *a*.

67. AGNOSTIC

The *agnostic* has not made up his mind and he claims, furthermore, that no man is capable of arriving at a conclusion as to whether or not there is a supreme being. *Agnostics* do not deny the existence of God—nor do they accept it. They state, simply, that they do not know, that nobody knows. Human knowledge, they say, is limited to actual human experience, hence they refuse to be convinced that revelation, spiritual experiences, or miracles prove divine existence. They are, in a sense, skeptics.

DEFINITION

An *agnostic*: neither accepts nor rejects the idea of God, claiming that humans are incapable of arriving at a conclusion as to divine existence.

PRONUNCIATIONS

Agnostic   ag-NOS'-tik
Agnosticism   ag-NOS'-tə-siz-əm

DERIVATION

Greek, *gnostos*, knowing, plus the negative Greek prefix *a*, not, hence *not knowing*.

68. CYNIC

You will recall the question discussed in Unit 12: Is man inherently good or evil? The *cynic* has an answer: Man is inherently evil, and any good he may display arises from evil motives. The *cynic* is usually distrustful, sneering, and contemptuous; he is almost always sarcastically skeptical of goodness, kindness, sincerity, morality, virtue, etc.

Paul is one of the most popular boys in his teenage set—obviously because he is likable, interesting, and considerate. But the *cynic* has a different attitude—Paul is popular because he has a new car; the other kids enjoy him not for himself but because he offers a means of locomotion to the gang.

Mrs. B. is a charming, vivacious, warm, and sympathetic woman. She is also a widow—and no longer young. However, she has a number of ardent suitors, all of whom seem to enjoy her company, a few of them apparently sincerely in love with her. Why? Again the *cynic* has a ready answer: her husband left her two million dollars.

DEFINITION

A *cynic*: is sneeringly contemptuous of goodness, morality, and the general sincerity of human motives.

PRONUNCIATIONS

Cynic	SIN´-ik
Cynical	SIN´-ə-kəl
Cynicism	SIN´-ə-siz-əm

DERIVATION

Greek *kynikos*, doglike, hence currish

69. CONNOISSEUR

The same Greek *gnostos, knowing*, found in *agnostic*, also appears in *connoisseur*, its altered form resulting from the changes that took place as this root traveled first to Latin and then to French, the language from which we directly borrowed the word.

In Latin, *gnostos* changed to *cognos*, and we see it in such common English words as *recognize* (know again) and *incognito* (unknown). When French words were built on this Latin (but originally Greek) root, the *g* was dropped, the French stem was spelled *connaiss* and was used to form the following words, all of them later borrowed by English: *reconnaissance* (an examination of a territory for military purposes to gain knowledge of the terrain, the inhabitants, etc.), *reconnoiter* (to make such a military examination of the territory), and *connoisseur*.

A *connoisseur*, then, by derivation, is a "knower."

And what does he know about? Art, music, foods, wine, beautiful women, and other pleasures of the senses.

The *connoisseur*'s information is trained knowledge. He knows a Botticelli from a Rembrandt, a Picasso from a Dali, and the elements of superiority of each of these painters. He knows the difference between a fugue, a symphony, and a tone poem, between champagne of a vintage year and a mediocre champagne. He knows when spaghetti is cooked exactly right, how to make the meat sauce perfect, what kinds of wines go with fish, fowl, and red meat. He is well-informed on feminine beauty, and can tell a blonde, brunette, or redhead how best to complement her distinctive coloring.

This is not to imply that a connoisseur is trained in *all* these fields. He may be a *connoisseur* of art, a *connoisseur* of music, a *connoisseur* of women, or a *connoisseur* of foods and wines. Often, of course, he is a *connoisseur* in all these related aspects of life, because he is a person with a profound knowledge and appreciation of, and a trained taste in, all that is beautiful—and in addition, is competent to act as a critical judge in most matters of esthetic appeal.

DEFINITION

A *connoisseur*: is someone who is esthetically versed in matters of art, taste, beauty, etc.

PRONUNCIATION

Connoisseur   kon-ə-SUR′

DERIVATION

French *connaître*, to know, indirectly from Latin and Greek.

70. LOTHARIO

You have perhaps met the type of man who attracts women like a magnet. He is probably tall, virile-looking, handsome, lively in conversation, chivalrous in nature, persevering in his attentions, and, perhaps most important, forthright and direct in his aims. His motives with a member of the opposite sex are clear-cut, unconcealed, and unvarying—and success generally attends his efforts.

However, his one lack, to which most women are blinded until too late, is sincerity. When (as the quaint saying goes) he has had his way with one woman, he is as likely as not to flit with unconcern to another.

The only accurate term for a man possessing this classic combination of physical and moral attributes is a *Lothario*. No other word quite fits.

DEFINITION

A *Lothario*: is a seducer, an unscrupulous rake.

PRONUNCIATION

Lothario   lō-THAIR′-ee-ō

DERIVATION

From the name of a character in an 18th-century British drama (*The Fair Penitent* by Nicholas Rowe) who combined the characteristics detailed above.

Test Your Learning

I. TRUE OR FALSE?

1. An *atheist* believes in God.	True	False
2. An *agnostic* denies the existence of God.	True	False
3. A *cynic* is contemptuous and distrustful of human motives.	True	False
4. A *connoisseur* is well versed in some esthetic field.	True	False
5. A *Lothario* generally has little, if any, success with women.	True	False

II. SAME OR OPPOSITE?

1. Atheist—believer	Same	Opposite
2. Agnostic—skeptic	Same	Opposite
3. Cynical—sneering	Same	Opposite
4. Connoisseur—judge	Same	Opposite
5. Lothario—seducer	Same	Opposite

III. USE THE WORD

1. You can't fool him with sparkling Burgundy—he's too much of a _____.
2. His _____ led him to reject all doctrines of revelation, but he never rejected outright the possibility of a supreme deity.
3. His _____ attitude to life makes him an uncomfortable person to confide in.
4. People who are outright _____ can rarely be convinced of forces greater than man.
5. Every summer resort boasts its share of _____.

IV. WRITE THE WORD

1. Seducer	1. _____
2. Distrustful of human motives	2. _____
3. Rejection of God	3. _____
4. Judge in matters of taste and art	4. _____
5. One who neither denies nor affirms the existence of a supreme being	5. _____

Check Your Learning

TEST I

1—true, 2—false, 3—true, 4—true, 5—false.

TEST II

1—opposite, 2—same, 3—same, 4—same, 5—same.

TEST III

1—connoisseur, 2—agnosticism, 3—cynical, 4—atheists, 5—Lotharios.

TEST IV

1—Lothario, 2—cynical, 3—atheism, 4—connoisseur, 5—agnostic.

Unit Fourteen

Thus far, then, we have discussed types of people who have varying attitudes to a supreme being (*atheists* and *agnostics*), who are distrustful of human motives (*cynics*), who are experts in matters of taste (*connoisseurs*), who have dynamic effects on women (*Lotharios*).

In the present Unit we shall discuss five new types, each of whom rides a different hobby or pursues a different interest.

71. NUMISMATIST

He collects coins, but not for the usual base and mercenary reasons. His interest in quarters, dimes, nickels and the rest is not in what he can buy with them—for to him metal money is not for the spending, but for the keeping. Nor does he limit himself to the coin of the realm, but is especially avid for old, rare, and unusual coins, of whatever shape or size and from whatever country.

The collection of such coins is the *numismatist*'s hobby, as is also the collection of old medals and other metal emblems. He is a devotee of the science of *numismatics*, and of course his *numismatic* knowledge is great—he can tell you the kind of coins and medals used by the ancient Romans and the modern Russians; how coins varied in different civilizations; how values changed from age to age. And, likely, he'll have a specimen of each of the types he refers to.

DEFINITION

Numismatist: a person whose hobby is the collection of coins and medals; one versed in the science of coins and medals.

PRONUNCIATIONS

Numismatist	nōō-MIZ'-mə-tist
Numismatic	nōō-məz-MAT'-ik
Numismatics	nōō-məz-MAT'-iks

DERIVATION

Latin *nomisma*, coin.

72. PHILATELIST

We have here a gentleman whose hobby is closely connected to that of the numismatist, whose interest is in postage stamps, cancellation stamps, stamped envelopes, post cards, and other such paraphernalia of the history of the mails, both current and historic, foreign as well as American. He is a *philatelist*.

Many great men (for example, Franklin D. Roosevelt) have relaxed with *philately*, which represents a thriving business. As in the case of coins, the *philatelic* value of a stamp is in direct ratio to its rarity.

DEFINITION

A *philatelist*: collects and studies stamps and other postal paraphernalia.

PRONUNCIATIONS

Philatelist	fə-LAT′-ə-list
Philatelic	fil′-ə-TEL′-ik
Philately	fə-LAT′-ə-lee

DERIVATION

Greek *philos*, love, plus *ateleia*, stamp.

73. BIBLIOPHILE

The hobby of the numismatist is coins, of the philatelist, postage stamps, and of the *bibliophile*, books. Not just any books, naturally, but first editions, rare volumes, old manuscripts, etc. The *bibliophile* is versed in the lore and history of old books, types of printing, methods of binding, and so on. *Bibliophilism* is a rich and intriguing hobby, and throws many interesting sidelights on the intellectual history of mankind; it is often a financially rewarding hobby, rare editions bringing fancy prices at auctions.

DEFINITION

Bibliophile: one who collects old books, etc.

PRONUNCIATIONS

Bibliophile	BIB′-lee-ə-fil′
Bibliophilism	bib′-lee-OF′-ə-liz-əm

Greek *biblios*, book, plus *philos*, love.

74. BALLETOMANE

The hobbies of the numismatist, philatelist, and bibliophile are fairly sedentary and intellectual pursuits. That of the *balletomane* is passive and sedentary enough, but more appealing to the senses than to the intellect. The *balletomane*'s enthusiasm is for the *ballet*, a special type of dance which tells an involved story, consists of intricate and expressive movements, and requires the greatest of artistic ability on the part of the dancer.

DEFINITION

Balletomane: a devotee of the ballet.

PRONUNCIATIONS

Balletomane	bə-LET'-ə-mayn'
Balletomania	bə-LET'-ə-may'-nee-ə

DERIVATION

Italian *ballo*, dance, in turn derived from Latin *ballare*, to dance. The English word *ball*, a social assembly for dancing, has the same source.

75. ANTIQUARIAN

Similarly passive, but somewhat more generalized, is the hobby of the *antiquarian*, who is interested in any of the relics of antiquity, be it old china, old books, old furniture, architectural remains, ancient instruments, early inventions.

What emotional experiences lead a person to collect articles of little functional value or intrinsic worth, the psychiatrists have not bothered to investigate to any great length, since collectors are harmless, socially acceptable, and fairly happy people. Their slight madness, whether it is manifested in coins, stamps, books, ballet-watching, or rare articles of any sort, does not inconvenience them or their friends to any great extent, and if they do not necessarily advance the progress of the world, certainly neither do they retard it.

DEFINITION

Antiquarian: a student and collector of antiquities.

PRONUNCIATIONS

Antiquarian	an'-tə-KWAIR'-ee-ən
Antiquarianism	an'-tə-KWAIR'-ee-ən-iz-əm

DERIVATION

Latin *antiquus*, old.

Test Your Learning

I. TRUE OR FALSE?

1. A *numismatist* collects stamps.   True   False
2. A *philatelist* collects coins.   True   False
3. A *bibliophile* is interested in books.   True   False
4. A *balletomane*'s greatest interest is the opera.   True   False
5. An *antiquarian* is interested in the products of bygone ages.   True   False

II. CHOOSE THEIR INTERESTS

If you met each of the hobbyists in Column I, decide on the topic of conversation, from those listed in Column II, which would elicit the greatest interest from him.

I	II
1. numismatist	a—first edition of Shakespeare
2. philatelist	b—spinning wheels
3. bibliophile	c—the waltz
4. balletomane	d—art of pantomime
5. antiquarian	e—diseases of old age
	f—postmarks
	g—Chinese money

III. CHANGE PARTS OF SPEECH

Change each word into its corresponding form to indicate the name of the hobby, science, or art.

1. numismatist
2. philatelist
3. bibliophile
4. balletomane
5. antiquarian

1. _____
2. _____
3. _____
4. _____
5. _____

IV. USE THE WORD

1. Franklin D. Roosevelt was an ardent _____; his stamp collection was priceless.

2. Along lower Fourth Avenue, in New York, you will find _____ poking in the dusty corners of the few remaining bookstores looking for rare volumes.

3. In rural Maine are many little roadside shops which cater to the interests of the _____ ; in each is a miscellaneous collection of antique furniture and implements.

4. The true _____ rarely misses a performance of Stravinsky's "Petrouchka" ballet.

5. The actual value of a coin is what it will buy over a counter; its _____ value, however, depends on its rarity, its condition, and the price a collector will pay for it.

V. WRITE THE WORD

1. Student and collector of objects of earlier ages
2. Stamp collector
3. Ballet enthusiast
4. Coin collector
5. Collector of rare books

1. _____
2. _____
3. _____
4. _____
5. _____

Check Your Learning

ANSWERS TO TESTS ON UNIT 14

TEST I
1—false, 2—false, 3—true, 4—false, 5—true.

TEST II
1—g, 2—f, 3—a, 4—d, 5—b or a.

TEST III
1—numismatics, 2—philately, 3—bibliophilism, 4—balletomania, 5—antiquarianism.

1—philatelist, 2—bibliophiles, 3—antiquarian, 4—balletomane, 5—numismatic.

1—antiquarian, 2—philatelist, 3—balletomane, 4—numismatist, 5—bibliophile.

Unit Fifteen

76. SADIST

Many, many years ago a man wrote a book, the story of his life, an account of his experiences with women. This was in the nineteenth century, and readers of that time did not have, in certain respects, the literary sophistication which we like to boast today. That is, they were not quite so shockproof.

The place was France, the author was the Marquis de Sade. Citizens of the present era might not be so overwhelmingly stirred up by the Marquis' autobiography as were the French in the early 1800s.

It must be admitted that the Marquis' work was unusual. His attitude toward women showed none of the tenderness and sentimentality generally associated with the French concept of love.

On the contrary, de Sade described in complete, frank, and intimate detail the cruelty and pain which he inflicted on the women he lured to his castle.

This cruelty was not, as you might suspect, of the spirit. It was, indeed, sheerly physical—it was bodily, anatomical pain that his companions in love suffered at the Marquis' hand. And the more they suffered, the greater was the Marquis' pleasure. Indeed, his *only* pleasure came from the pain of others.

Such an attitude is, of course, abnormal, diseased, perverted. But it is not unique. And so out of the Marquis' name was coined a word—*sadism*—which at first described the neurotic sexual pleasure derived by sick minds from inflicting physical pain on partners in the love act.

Originally, then, the term *sadist* was a highly restricted one—but gradually the meaning of the word was extended to areas beyond the sexual, and today a *sadist* is anyone whose pleasure comes from another's pain. That pain may be physical, spiritual, mental, moral—and so may the pleasure.

The little boy whose savage delight it is to tear the wings off flies, to mutilate his pets, to torture his baby sister, has tendencies which may be called *sadistic*. The district attorney who ecstatically makes the unhappy witness writhe in mental agony, no less than the happy detectives who torture a defenseless prisoner, may accurately be termed *sadistic*. And the Nazi storm troopers slowly and painfully killing their victims, no more than the merciless husband purposefully driving his wife to the border of insanity with mental cruelty, may aptly be accused of *sadism*.

The *sadist*, then, in any realm, sexual or otherwise, derives his greatest pleasure from inflicting pain, from being the cause of other people's misery.

DEFINITION

Sadist: one whose chief pleasure comes from inflicting pain on others.

PRONUNCIATIONS

Sadist	SAY'-dist *or* SAD'-ist
Sadism	SAY'-diz-am *or* SAD'-iz-əm
Sadistic	sa-DIS'-tik

DERIVATION

French, from the Marquis de Sade.

77. MASOCHIST

Somewhat later in the nineteenth century, Leopold von Sacher-Masoch, an Austrian, wrote a novel, *Venus in Fur*. This book portrayed characters whose pleasure from the opposite sex was derived in a very different manner from that of the Frenchman, de Sade; characters who were happy only if they suffered, rather than inflicted, pain, only if they submitted to humiliation, cruelty, or torture. The mania of Sacher-Masoch's imaginary people was, though neurotic, diseased, and perverted, far from unique—and the Austrian's name was used to coin *masochism*, a term now applied to the weird and abnormal pleasure which some emotionally sick people derive from suffering physical, mental, or spiritual pain in the sexual or in any other area.

The *masochist* is the opposite number, the converse, of the sadist. A person of *masochistic* tendencies is most ecstatic, if you will permit the paradox, when he is most miserable. His misery may be inflicted upon him by others, or it may be self-generated, but whatever the source, however it is manifested (physical agony, humiliation, mental cruelty, embarrassment) it is sheer delight.

Psychiatry recognizes that *masochism* may to a great extent be unconscious. The *masochist*, that is, does not consciously realize that inner forces of his personality impel him to seek disgrace, avoidable hardships, unnecessary troubles; nor is he aware that only when he seeks and finds such misery and unhappiness is he completely (and unconsciously) gratified.

Contrary to the generality of normal, pleasure-seeking humanity, the *masochist* is the pain-seeker—pain, his own pain, is his finest pleasure, conscious or unconscious. The woman who marries a drunkard perhaps realizing unconsciously that her life with him will be unbearable; the mother who is so self-sacrificing for her children that she humiliates them as well as herself; the man who invariably finds the most difficult and painful way of getting things done, or who sets for himself clearly unattainable goals, so that he can be miserable when he fails to attain them—these types are *masochistic*.

Look around you, look deeply into the behavior of your friends and acquaintances—you may be surprised at how many of them are *masochistic*, either to a slight or pronounced degree.

DEFINITION

Masochist: one who, consciously or unconsciously, seeks and is gratified by unnecessary pain or humiliation.

PRONUNCIATIONS

Masochist	MAS′-ə-kist
Masochism	MAS′-ə-kiz-əm
Masochistic	mas′-ə-KIS′-tik

DERIVATION

From the Austrian, Leopold von Sacher-Masoch.

78. VOLUPTUARY

As you can see, there are pleasures of various sorts, and arising from various sources. The sadist's pleasure comes from cruelty, the masochist's from his own pain and suffering. There are those who derive the finest and noblest of pleasures from an austere life, from religious experiences, from self-denials; there are others whose deepest delight springs from intellectual stimulation, or from emotional warmth, or from feelings of accomplishment or self-realization.

And there are also the *voluptuaries*. For them, pleasure comes from luxurious gratification of the senses—and for them, the ideal life is one spent in the pursuit of such sensuous pleasures.

"Luxurious gratification of the senses"—let us examine the significance and implications of that phrase.

The five senses, as we know, are taste, touch, hearing, smell, and sight. And so the *voluptuary* gets a tremendous, and ecstatic, gratification from rich food and mellow liquors (taste); from expensive garments, beautiful blondes, warm baths, Swedish massages, lying in the sun (touch); well-played music, the opera, sultry songs (hearing); flowers, perfumes, the bouquets of wines, the spices of foods (smell); sunsets, the reflection of the moon on the water, a curvaceous young girl, the pageantry of the theater, paintings and sculpture and scenery and seascapes (sight).

But this is only part of the story.

You and I can enjoy the things I have listed, and many similar to them, without being *voluptuaries*.

The *voluptuary*'s pleasure in these sensuous stimulants (this is one of the two important distinctions) is richly emotional, uninhibited, unashamed, unthinned by moral, ethical, or intellectual factors; his reaction to them is that of a person intoxicated.

In addition, while you and I may enjoy these things when we meet them, and be equally able to enjoy spiritual or intellectual things, the *voluptuary* dedicates his life to the pursuit and enjoyment of sensuous pleasures (this is the second distinction).

In short, the *voluptuary* is one to whom delights of the senses are intoxicating, and for whom little else in life has the same importance.

DEFINITION

Voluptuary: one who makes gratification of the senses his chief aim in life.

PRONUNCIATION

Voluptuary   və-LUP'-choo-air-ee

DERIVATION

Latin *voluptas*, pleasure.

79. COQUETTE

The *coquette* is a teaser, a tantalizer. She promises much, everything, and at the final moment delivers little, nothing. She is a flirt, a female Lothario who will go only so far. She tries to gain the amorous admiration and affections of men merely to delight her vanity; she is insincere, often unattainable. And (this is most important) her own affections and emotions are rarely, if ever, involved.

What are the weapons of her *coquetry?* The playful glance, the suggestive pose or gesture, the implied (but never directly expressed) promise. *Coquettish* attitudes and behavior were more popular in an earlier generation than today. Now women can afford to be direct, sincere, and forthright, both in their acceptance and in their refusal.

DEFINITION

Coquette: an insincere flirt.

PRONUNCIATIONS

Coquette	kō-KET'
Coquetry	KŌ-kə-tree
Coquettish	kō-KET'-ish

DERIVATION

French, *coq*, a cock, a strutting rooster.

80. CHARLATAN

He may be a doctor who claims to be able to cure diseases against which he is, in truth, powerless. He may be a self-styled psychologist who, knowing nothing of psychology or any of the allied sciences, pretends to be able to cure emotional disorders or give helpful advice. He may be any person who tries to fool the public by putting on a show of knowledge or skill which he does not possess. In other words, he's an imposter, a faker, a fraud, and a cheat—such is the *charlatan*.

In general use, the term *charlatan* is applied only to those fakers and impostors who pretend that they can help people in distress, but whose suggestions or remedies come not from knowledge, skill, or training, but purely from ignorance, self-delusion, or outright attempts at deception.

DEFINITION

Charlatan: one who pretends to knowledge which he does not possess.

PRONUNCIATIONS

Charlatan	SHAHR′-lə-tən
Charlatanism	SHAHR′-lə-tən-iz-əm
Charlatanic	shahr′-lə-TAN′-ik

DERIVATION

Italian, *ciarlatano*, a seller of counterfeit papal indulgences.

Test Your Learning

I. TRUE OR FALSE?

1. A *sadist* is kind and gentle.	True	False
2. A *masochist* is self-indulgent.	True	False
3. A *voluptuary* leads a life of self-denial.	True	False
4. A *coquette* is a hypocrite.	True	False
5. A *charlatan* is trustworthy.	True	False

II. SAME OR OPPOSITE?

1. Sadistic—cruel	Same	Opposite
2. Masochistic—pain-loving	Same	Opposite
3. Voluptuary—pleasure-seeking	Same	Opposite
4. Coquettish—flirtatious	Same	Opposite
5. Charlatanic—fraudulent	Same	Opposite

III. USE THE WORD

1. That man may have a great reputation for curing cancer, but I know many doctors who privately accuse him of _____.
2. The two brothers are amazingly different. One is ascetic, austere, dour, self-denying; the other is an out-and-out _____.
3. Somehow, _____ ally, he always got himself into a position of being humiliated, scorned, rejected. Then, and only then, was he satisfied.
4. It did not take a man very long to discover that she was just a _____.
5. He was a victim of the ruthless _____ of one of the most savage of the Nazis.

IV. WRITE THE WORD

1. Insincere flirtatiousness
2. Pleasure derived from one's own pain
3. Pretense to a knowledge that one does not possess
4. A seeker after sensuous pleasures
5. Happiness from inflicing pain on others

1. _____
2. _____
3. _____
4. _____
5. _____

Check Your Learning

ANSWERS TO TESTS ON UNIT 15

TEST I

1—false, 2—false, 3—false, 4—true, 5—false.

TEST II

1—same, 2—same, 3—same, 4—same, 5—same.

TEST III

1—charlatanism, 2—voluptuary, 3—masochistic(ally), 4—coquette, 5—sadism.

TEST IV

1—coquetry, 2—masochism, 3—charlatanism, 4—voluptuary, 5—sadism.

Unit Sixteen

81. THESPIAN

It is believed that the drama as we know it in modern times was founded some twenty-four hundred years ago in ancient Greece. The big wheel in theater circles at that time, a sort of early day John Houseman or Stephen Sondheim, was the poet Thespis—and so today we often call any actor or actress, especially (though not exclusively) one who plays tragic roles, a *thespian*.

(Thespis was a kind of all-round handyman in the theater. He wrote the poetic dramas, managed the company, trained the chorus, transported the properties—on a cart—from place to place, and acted in his own plays.)

Thespian is, of course, an over-elegant term for actor, and so is often employed humorously, in mild contempt, or to lend mock dignity to the profession. However, the word may be, and occasionally is, used seriously, neutrally, and with no derogatory connotation.

DEFINITION

Thespian: an actor or actress.

PRONUNCIATION

Thespian   THES'-pee-ən

DERIVATION

From the Greek poet Thespis, reputedly the founder of Greek drama.

82. TERPSICHOREAN

In Greek mythology, Terpsichore (pronounced turp-SICK-er-ee) was the muse of dancing and choral singing. A muse, according to mythology, was one of the nine daughters of the god Zeus (ZOOS) and the goddess Mnemosyne (ne-MOSS-i-nee), and each presided over, inspired, and protected one of the important fields (then so considered) of human endeavor. Calliope (ka-LYE-o-pee) was the muse of heroic poetry; Clio (KLEE-o), of history; Erato (ERR-a-to), of love poetry; Euterpe (yoo-TUR-pee), of music and lyric poetry; Melpomene (mell-POM-e-nee), of tragedy; Polymnia (po-LIM-nee-a), of sacred hymns; Terpsichore, as we have said, of dancing and choral singing; Thalia (tha-LYE-a), of comedy and idyllic poetry; and Urania (yoo-RAY-nee-a), of astronomy.

Of these nine, only two have been perpetuated in the English language: Terpsichore and Calliope. A *terpsichorean* is a dancer, and a calliope is a mobile steam organ, generally found today in circuses. The names of the other muses have been obscured by time, and the only value of knowing them, I suppose, is to win a washing machine or refrigerator on a TV game show or, perhaps, to impress your less learned friends.

Terpsichorean, like thespian, often has a humorous or mock-heroic connotation; but both words are frequently found in writing about the theater.

DEFINITION

Terpsichorean: a dancer.

PRONUNCIATION

Terpsichorean   turp′-sə-kə-REE′-ən

DERIVATION

From Terpsichore, muse of the dance.

83. CHOREOGRAPHER

In Greek the root *choreia* means dance, the root *graphein* means to write. A *choreographer* then, by derivation, is one who writes dances. Today, the word has been restricted to that person whose profession it is to arrange dances for the ballet form, and when you see, in the theater program of a musical comedy, "*Choreography* by Twyla Tharp" for example, you know that Miss Tharp arranged, supervised, and directed the ballet numbers.

DEFINITION

Choreographer: arranger of ballet numbers.

Choreographer   kawr′-ee-OG′-rə-fər
Choreography   kawr′-ee-OG′-rə-fee
Choreographic   kawr′-ee-ə-GRAF′-ik

DERIVATION

Greek *choreia*, dance, plus *graphein*, to write.

84. NAIAD

Drawing again upon classical mythology, as English so often does, we find that the ancient Greeks believed that most things in the world were under the special protection of divine or semi-divine forms. Each god and goddess had a particular province, and any human being expecting to be successful in that province had best see to it that the presiding deity was on his side. Even parts of the earth were so protected, and certain water-nymphs were in charge of various springs, streams, brooks, etc. These nymphs, though not true goddesses, had of course supernatural origin and powers, and if a stream dried up or overflowed, there was, so the Greeks believed, no natural cause, but rather the playfulness or caprice of its presiding *naiad*.

And so, to propitiate the *naiads*, the Greeks would sacrifice goats and lambs to them, and offer milk, fruit, flowers, oil, honey, and wine as bribes for the nymphs' good will.

(In addition to the *naiads*, the other nymphs, all possessed of eternal youth, were the *oreads* (OR-ee-ad) who controlled hills and mountains; the *nereids* (NEER-ee-id), who presided over the sea; the *dryads* (DRY-ad), who were in charge of the woods and trees; and the *oceanids* (o-SEE-a-nid), who held sway over the oceans.)

Today we sometimes use the term *naiad* to refer to a woman swimmer, usually one who, like the ancient *naiads*, is most at home in the water.

DEFINITION

Naiad: a woman swimmer.

PRONUNCIATION

Naiad   NAY′-ad′

Greek *naiad*, a water-nymph.

85. NIMROD

English words come from divers and strange sources. *Naiad, thespian,* and *terpsichorean,* as we have seen, are from Greek mythology, and *choreographer* from two Greek roots; *nimrod* derives from the name of a man in Biblical times, Nimrod, the son of Cush and grandson of Ham, who was the ruler of the city of Babel. A line in Genesis describes Nimrod, in passing, as "a mighty hunter," and today any devotee of hunting may be described by this term. Like *thespian, terpsichorean,* and *naiad, nimrod* is a literary allusion, and a word more found in print than heard in everyday conversation.

DEFINITION

Nimrod: a hunter.

PRONUNCIATION

Nimrod   NIM-rod'

DERIVATION

From a name in the Bible, book of Genesis.

Test Your Learning

I. TRUE OR FALSE?

1. A *thespian* is a dramatist.   True   False
2. A *terpsichorean* is an actor.   True   False
3. A *choreographer* is a ballet dancer.   True   False
4. A *naiad* is a girl swimmer.   True   False
5. A *nimrod* is a hunter.   True   False

II. MATCH WORDS AND INTERESTS

I	II
1. Thespian	a—swimming
2. Terpsichorean	b—ballet arrangements
3. Choreographer	c—singing

4. Naiad   d—fishing
5. Nimrod   e—acting
              f—hunting
              g—dancing

III. APPLY THE WORD

Which word would most closely fit each of the following people?

1. Twyla Tharp   1. _____
2. Daniel Boone   2. _____
3. Esther Williams   3. _____
4. Nijinsky, Fred Astaire   4. _____
5. John Barrymore, Maurice Evans   5. _____

IV. WRITE THE WORD

1. A dancer   1. _____
2. An actor   2. _____
3. A girl swimmer   3. _____
4. A hunter   4. _____
5. A ballet arranger   5. _____

Check Your Learning

ANSWERS TO TESTS ON UNIT 16

TEST I

1—false, 2—false, 3—false, 4—true, 5—true.

TEST II

1—e, 2—g, 3—b, 4—a, 5—f.

TEST III

1—choreographer, 2—nimrod, 3—naiad, 4—terpsichorean, 5—thespian.

TEST IV

1—terpsichorean, 2—thespian, 3—naiad, 4—nimrod, 5—choreographer.

Review Test IV

I. MATCHING

A.

1. Atheist   a—suspects human motives
2. Cynic   b—collects stamps
3. Lothario   c—inflicts cruelty
4. Philatelist   d—makes love to women
5. Balletomane   e—is devoted to pleasure

6. Sadist   f—is a dancer
7. Voluptuary   g—denies God
8. Charlatan   h—is a woman swimmer
9. Terpsichorean   i—pretends to skill or knowledge he does not
10. Naiad   have
                       j—is devoted to the ballet

B.

1. Agnostic   a—a judge of taste or value
2. Connoisseur   b—flirt
3. Numismatist   c—book-collector
4. Bibliophile   d—enjoys self-inflicted pain
5. Antiquarian   e—arranges music for ballet dancing
6. Masochist   f—expert in relics of the past
7. Coquette   g—actor
8. Thespian   h—coin collector
9. Choreographer   i—a hunter
10. Nimrod   j—believes there may or may not be a God

II. CHANGE PARTS OF SPEECH

1. Atheist—a believer in _____.
2. Agnostic—an adherent of _____.
3. Cynic—his constant _____.
4. Numismatist—well-versed in the field of _____.
5. Philatelist—an encyclopedia of _____.
6. Sadist—his _____ urges.
7. Masochist—her _____ tendencies.
8. Coquette—an expert in the art of _____.
9. Charlatan—accused of _____.
10. Choreographer—a patron of the _____ arts.

III. WRITE THE WORD

For each key idea write the word of Part IV which most aptly fits. As a true test, do not refer to previous lists.

1. Swimming   1. _____
2. Stamps   2. _____
3. Cruelty to others   3. _____
4. Old things   4. _____
5. Judge   5. _____
6. Godlessness   6. _____
7. Flirting   7. _____
8. Pretense of knowledge   8. _____
9. Ballet arranging   9. _____

10. Hunting   10. _____
11. Ballet attending   11. _____
12. Making love to women   12. _____
13. Skepticism about God   13. _____
14. Acting   14. _____
15. Dancing   15. _____
16. Coins   16. _____
17. Skepticism about goodness   17. _____
18. Enjoyment of pain   18. _____
19. Pursuit of pleasure   19. _____
20. Books   20. _____

Check Your Learning

ANSWERS TO REVIEW TEST IV

TEST IA

1—g, 2—a, 3—d, 4—b, 5—j, 6—c, 7—e, 8—i, 9—f, 10—h.

TEST IB

1—j, 2—a, 3—h, 4—c, 5—f, 6—d, 7—b, 8—g, 9—e, 10—i.

TEST II

1—atheism, 2—agnosticism, 3—cynicism, 4—numismatics, 5—philately, 6—sadistic, 7—masochistic, 8—coquetry, 9—charlatanism, 10—choreographic.

TEST III

1—naiad, 2—philatelist, 3—sadist, 4—antiquarian, 5—connoisseur, 6—atheist, 7—coquette, 8—charlatan, 9—choreographer, 10—nimrod, 11—balletomane, 12—Lothario, 13—agnostic, 14—thespian, 15—terpsichorean, 16—numismatist, 17—cynic, 18—masochist, 19—voluptuary, 20—bibliophile.

PART V

Things

Note these phrases:
1. A *perfunctory* examination
2. A *facetious* remark
3. A *veracious* report
4. *Wanton* cruelty
5. An *illicit* meeting
6. *Licentious* behavior
7. *Prodigious* strength
8. *Obsolete* armament
9. *Sacrilegious* act
10. *Resonant* tones
11. *Dissonant* chords
12. *Desultory* reading
13. *Auspicious* beginning
14. *Precarious* profession
15. A *spurious* claim
16. *Dilatory* tactics
17. *Incongruous* appearance

How many of these phrases do you completely understand?

How many of the italicized words could you use successfully, meaningfully, effectively?

Read on . . .

Unit Seventeen

86. PERFUNCTORY

When you do something, you can put your whole heart in it. You can be inspired, aiming at perfection, loving every minute of your work, unable to tear yourself away from your job until it is complete in every detail, and regretful when you have finished.

Or you can be very different. You can do something mechanically, superficially, just to be able to say you have done it, but with no care or interest, and with such an air of tedium that no one can mistake your resistance and inner unwillingness.

There's your contrast.

Watch a child at play. Notice how rapt he is, how oblivious to outside noises and happenings. Then watch the same child performing a task forced on him by his parents: picking at food he doesn't like, cleaning his room, washing the car, clearing the table, etc. In the latter activities he merely goes through the motions, does just enough to be able to claim that he has complied with the parental order.

Do something in a *perfunctory* manner, and you merely go through the motions, nothing more. No real interest, no desire, no care, no great willingness, just get it done and get it over with.

You are telling someone about your troubles—but he has his own troubles on his mind. He is listening, but it is obvious that he doesn't hear. You can say that he listens *perfunctorily*, gives your words only *perfunctory* attention, exhibits *perfunctory* interest in what you are saying.

An author brings his precious manuscript to an editor, who, however, has more important things to think of that day. The editor leafs through the pages *perfunctorily*, her mind obviously far away.

A busy doctor may give his patient a *perfunctory* examination, someone may show *perfunctory* courtesy to a subordinate, or send a *perfunctory* letter of thanks to Aunt Suzy for a useless wedding present. Or a wife may be irritated by the *perfunctoriness* of her husband's interest when she recounts to him, after he has lived through a hard day at his office, the difficulties she had at work.

Perfunctory means: performed merely as a routine and uninteresting
  duty; mechanical, uninspired, careless; going through the motions,
  but reluctantly and unhappily.

PRONUNCIATIONS

Perfunctory	pər-FUNK′-tə-ree
Perfunctorily	pər-FUNK′-tə-rə-lee
Perfunctoriness	pər-FUNK′-tə-ree-nəss

DERIVATION

Latin, *perfunctum*, performed.

87. FACETIOUS

Humor, says one psychoanalytic school of thought, is based on hostility.
In a social gathering, for instance, the person who feels the most hostility
(conscious or unconscious) to the world will be the one who tries hardest
to make the funny remarks (generally at someone else's expense), who
will seem to get the greatest fun out of causing discomfort to others,
whether by sarcasm, verbal taunts, or practical jokes. This is his way
of masking his hostility while simultaneously, but indirectly, releasing
it. And generally no one so fully enjoys his antics as does he himself.

   You can usually stand just so much of such a character. His habit
of saying just the opposite of what you think he means tends finally to
bore and irritate.

   One of his principal weapons is *facetiousness.* He will indulge in levity
when it is least appropriate, his attempts at wit please him more than
his listeners, he is often described by his friends as "a great kidder."

   Facetious describes wit or humor in circumstances where seriousness
is required. It describes a person who shies away from truth or frankness
by making a silly remark, by retreating into a frivolous attitude. It
describes a personality who will not face reality, who prefers the indirect
and humorous approach, the witty and evasive answer, the escape by
a pun or obviously foolish and purposely pointless statement.

   Facetious is a term of mild contempt and irritation. "Stop being
facetious," "Don't be so *facetious,*" and "Your *facetiousness* won't help
you any this time" are statements which show our annoyance. People
of emotional maturity are rarely *facetious,* for *facetiousness* is a means

of evasion (through humor). The immature person, on the other hand, may wax *facetious* at the slightest provocation. Not all immature people are *facetious*, of course—there are other, less subtle, means of evasion, of refusing to face reality. But the constantly *facetious* person is very likely to be immature, insecure, and probably unhappy.

DEFINITION

Facetious means: characterized by inappropriate humor or levity; "kidding."

PRONUNCIATIONS

Facetious	fə-SEE′-shəs
Facetiously	fə-SEE′-shəs-lee
Facetiousness	fə-SEE′-shəs-nəs

DERIVATION

Latin *facetus*, witty, humorous.

88. VERACIOUS

Truth is, admittedly, a subject of philosophic discussion, but under ordinary circumstances there is a clear distinction between fact and fancy, between truthfulness and falsity, between honesty and dishonesty.

A story, an account, a statement, or any expression of words which adheres to facts, which respects the truth, which is honest and aboveboard, may be termed *veracious*. A person who is habitually truthful, whose word one can trust, may be called *veracious*. *Veracity* is a quality typical of people who habitually respect the truth, and when you doubt someone's *veracity* you are implying that you are not sure of his general honesty. A story which has the ring of *veracity* sounds as if it were told by a person whose habit it is to be truthful.

DEFINITION

Veracious means: accurate, honest, characterized by truth.

PRONUNCIATIONS

Veracious	və-RAY′-shəs
Veracity	və-RAS′-ə-tee

Latin *verus*, true.

89. MENDACIOUS

As veracious implies the habit of truthfulness, so *mendacious* implies habitual falsehood. A *mendacious* account is dishonest, untruthful, and intended to deceive; its author is probably a habitual liar. Accuse a person of *mendacity* and you mean not only that he is telling a lie, but also that he lies more often than not, that this one lie is typical rather than special.

DEFINITION

Mendacious means: given to falsehood.

PRONUNCIATIONS

Mendacious	men-DAY'-shəs
Mendacity	men-DAS'-ə-tee

DERIVATION

Latin *mendax*, lying.

90. WANTON

There are people in this world, as you no doubt know, who seem unhampered by conscience, ethical standards, moral restrictions, or the slightest iota of considerations for the feelings of others.

It would be a mistake to consider such people emotionally free or uninhibited, much as their actions may seem uncontrolled and unrestricted. This is a seeming paradox, perhaps, but one that can be explained.

The truly free and uninhibited personality is rarely the victim of his own hostility, rarely is at the mercy of his unconscious need to hurt others, to be cruel or reckless. An inhibition, according to the psychiatric use of the word, is an inability, psychologically, to do the things one wants to do; denying oneself an outlet to normal desires, one often commits acts of aggression, hostility, or cruelty as a kind of compensation, a sort of indirect satisfaction of desires long suppressed.

Let me be specific. Owing to childhood sexual inhibitions placed on him by his parents, a man is unable to develop a warm, normal, outgoing relationship with a member of the opposite sex. Hence, he feels frustrated, held in, denied he knows not what by forces he does not begin to understand.

Unconsciously, he rebels—against himself, against women, against the world. He seems to be saying, without putting the feeling into words, "I cannot relate to people, and it can't be my fault, it must be that people hate me. I don't care what I do to people, or to myself. I'll be reckless, cruel, aggressive, destructive." And he is; though actually he is most inhibited—deep down, concealed. His freedom is a sham and a pretense, but so artfully camouflaged that it deceives not only the world, but himself too.

An emotionally free person relates well to others and to himself. He has no need to punish the world, to take reckless chances, to get even. His outlets can be normal, and he is considerate not because he forces himself to be, but because he has no need to hurt anyone.

This explanation is intended as a background of understanding of the true motives of those people whose actions appear contemptuous of the feelings of others, of justice or kindness, who are cruel and destructive seemingly without just provocation or motive.

Such people, such actions, are most accurately described by the adjective *wanton*.

Any inconsiderate or hurtful act, apparently unprovoked and unmotivated, or motivated on the surface by pure malice, is a *wanton* act.

You have heard stories of the *wanton* cruelty of certain armies; how the soldiers, uncontrolled, killed children, raped women, burned and destroyed properties. No military purpose was served, no provocation can explain the senseless violence. It was *wanton*.

You have heard, also, of the *wanton* violence of a mob, the *wanton* bombing of defenseless civilians by enemy planes, the *wanton* cruelty of the Nazi storm troopers, or, in an earlier time, the *wanton* destruction of life by the Russian Cossacks.

And nature, too, can commit *wanton* destruction by earthquakes, tidal waves, volcanic eruptions, hurricanes.

There is another meaning to *wanton*, somewhat connected, and springing from the same unconscious hostility. Here *wanton* refers to sexual depravity, and a *wanton* woman is (superficially) uncontrolled in her appetites and promiscuity. (Actually, in many instances, she is unconsciously getting back at cold or overrestrictive parents. Rarely does a delinquent girl come from a home where there is warmth, security, and affection.)

Wanton may also be used as a noun, a synonym for a sexually depraved, promiscuous, and uncontrolled woman. To play the *wanton* is to act like such a woman.

DEFINITION

Wanton means: marked by arrogant contempt for justice and the feelings of others; unprovoked, unmotivated, wilfully malicious.

PRONUNCIATIONS

Wanton	WAHN'-tən
Wantonness	WAHN'-tən-əs

DERIVATION

Anglo-Saxon *wantoun*, of similar meaning.

Test Your Learning

I. TRUE OR FALSE?

1. A *perfunctory* answer is one resulting from careful thought.   True   False
2. A *facetious* remark is intended to be humorous.   True   False
3. A *veracious* account is truthful.   True   False
4. Accuse a man of *mendacity* and you imply that he is a habitual liar.   True   False
5. *Wanton* cruelty is purposeless.   True   False

II. SAME OR OPPOSITE?

1. Perfunctory—mechanical   Same   Opposite
2. Facetious—serious   Same   Opposite
3. Veracious—false   Same   Opposite
4. Mendacious—truthful   Same   Opposite
5. Wanton—considerate   Same   Opposite

III. USE THE WORDS

1. The reply was so full of contradictions and inconsistencies that it was obviously _____.
2. The auditors made a _____ examination of the books, for they were certain the bank was honestly run.
3. He is generally so _____ that you never know what he is really thinking.

4. No one doubts his _____ but the story is nevertheless hard to believe.

5. The firebug was indicted for _____ destruction of property.

IV. WRITE THE WORD

1. Flip or frivolous at times when seriousness is required.   1. _____

2. Untruthfulness   2. _____

3. Honesty in utterances   3. _____

4. Senseless, unprovoked, inconsiderate   4. _____

5. Mechanical, superficial, showing no interest, merely going through the motions.   5. _____

Check Your Learning

ANSWERS TO TESTS ON UNIT 17

TEST I

1—false, 2—true, 3—true, 4—true, 5—true.

TEST II

1—same, 2—opposite, 3—opposite, 4—opposite, 5—opposite.

TEST III

1—mendacious, 2—perfunctory, 3—facetious, 4—veracity, 5—wanton.

TEST IV

1—facetious, 2—mendacity, 3—veracity, 4—wanton, 5—perfunctory.

Unit Eighteen

91. ILLICIT

There is a verb in Latin which means *to permit*—namely, *licere*. This is the root from which comes our English word *license*, which obviously is a permit to do something, such as get married, drive a car, or own a dog. (Realizing that *license* derives from *licere*, you will not be tempted to misspell it *liscence*.)

If something is permitted, then, it is *licensed* or, which is a rarely used word in English, *licit*, from the same verb *licere*.

In, as you know, is a Latin prefix with a negative force; when it precedes a root beginning with *l*, the *n* changes to *l* for smoother pronunciation. *Licit* plus *in* thus becomes *illicit*, *not permitted*.

Strictly, *illicit* means *unlawful*, *illegal*, but it has, usually, a special and distinguishing connotation.

Exceeding the speed limit in a car is illegal and unlawful, but not *illicit;* a law is being violated, but there is no question of morals, convention, or propriety involved.

On the other hand, adultery,* which is illegal and considered immoral, can be termed *illicit*, and so we may speak of an *illicit* relationship between two people, one of whom is married to a third person; of an *illicit* rendezvous; an *illicit* affair; an *illicit* meeting, etc.

Trafficking in drugs such as opium, heroin, and other narcotics is also illegal, and again a question of vice or morals is involved; so we may speak of *illicit* purchases of opium, *illicit* sale of cocaine, *illicit* growing of marijuana, and the like.

An act is *illicit*, then, if it is not only illegal but also in violation of established moral conduct or sexual propriety, involved in vice, etc. *Illicit* is a more stigmatizing word than *illegal*, more indicative of society's disapproval.

DEFINITION

Illicit means: unlawful and improper.

*See Unit 23.

Illicit	il-IS'-ət
Illicitly	il-IS'-ət-lee
Illicitness	il-IS'-ət-nəs

DERIVATION

Latin *licere*, to permit, plus negative prefix *in*.

92. LICENTIOUS

Sex, as you doubtless realize, is the one area of living over which parents, society, the state, and the law attempt to exercise the greatest control. Any sexual acts or habits which violate such common restraints, which disregard the customs and laws of chastity, take license or permission beyond that allowed by law, morality, and convention—such acts or habits are termed *licentious*. We may speak of *licentious* behavior, meaning loose, lewd, unrestrained behavior; *licentious* living, *licentious* conduct; or *licentious* books and writings, namely those intended to inflame desire.

DEFINITION

Licentious means: loose, lewd, unrestrained, in violation of sexual morality.

PRONUNCIATIONS

Licentious	lī-SEN'-shəs
Licentiously	lī-SEN'-shəs-lee
Licentiousness	lī-SEN'-shəs-nəs

DERIVATION

Latin *Licere*, permit.

93. PRODIGIOUS

An old, and now rarely used, meaning of the word *prodigy* is a wonder that is out of the usual course of nature—for example, an eclipse of the sun, the raining of manna from heaven, the parting of the Red Sea, a snowstorm in mid-summer, a heat wave in January, etc. Today *prodigy* is largely restricted either to children whose mental or musical gifts depart markedly from the course of human nature, as a mathematical *prodigy*, a violin *prodigy*, a musical *prodigy*, a child *prodigy*, etc.; or to human actions astonishingly beyond general and accustomed abilities, as *prodigies* of valor, *prodigies* of courage, endurance, strength, and the like.

From the noun *prodigy* is formed the adjective *prodigious*, whose meaning naturally extends to describe anything extraordinary in size, bulk, degree, or force; anything which is marvelous beyond belief or entirely out of proportion to what is expected. We may therefore speak of the *prodigious* demand for gasoline and steel during the Second World War; a *prodigious* bestseller; *prodigious* good (or bad) luck; *prodigious* drive for power; *prodigious* strength; *prodigious* heat or cold; *prodigious* capacity for work; *prodigious* feasting; *prodigious* noise, and so on. You can work *prodigiously*, eat *prodigiously*, be a *prodigious* lover, build a *prodigious* number of houses, or amass a *prodigious* fortune. If it's *prodigious*, it's breathtaking, amazing, incredible, stupendous, colossal, awe-inspiring, etc. etc. etc.

DEFINITION

Prodigious means: extraordinary and astonishing in size, force, extent, etc.

PRONUNCIATIONS

Prodigious	prə-DIJ'-əs
Prodigiously	prə-DIJ'-əs-lee
Prodigiousness	prə-DIJ'-əs-nəs

DERIVATION

Latin *prodigium*, a prodigy.

94. PRODIGAL

Nature is notoriously *prodigal*—a salmon lays millions of eggs, though only a few survive to develop into little salmons; the human ovum is fertilized by a single sperm, but millions of spermatozoa are produced; a tree or flower drops millions of seeds, an infinitesimal fraction of which ever take root. Is all the rest waste? Perhaps from a certain point of view it is, but nature has her own secret designs and purposes.

Humans also are too often *prodigal*. In the early days of this country, natural resources of timber, topsoil, and various minerals were used with such *prodigality* that without rigorous conservation certain areas would today be bare of substance (many areas, indeed, are already ruined beyond hope of conservation), and various regions have been attacked, or are in constant danger of being attacked, by dust storms. Vast deserts in Asia attest to man's *prodigality* in prehistoric times.

Prodigality, then, is extravagant and wasteful use of what one has with no thought of the morrow. One may be *prodigal* of one's financial resources (traveling salesmen and thieves are noted for the *prodigal* way in which they squander their money when they have it, their *prodigal* manner of living while the money is coming in, their complete destitution at other times), of one's talents, of one's affections, etc. The *prodigal* is an excellent example of feast today, famine tomorrow—quite the opposite of the frugal person. When you live *prodigally* you are recklessly extravagant, lavishly wasteful, drunk with spending. It's probably a wonderful sensation while it lasts—but be prepared for the hangover when it's gone. And it's gone all too soon when you are truly *prodigal*.

DEFINITION

Prodigal means: extravagantly wasteful.

PRONUNCIATIONS

Prodigal	PROD'-ə-gəl
Prodigally	PROD'-ə-gə-lee
Prodigality	prod'-ə-GAL-ə-tee

DERIVATION

Latin *prodigere*, to squander.

USAGE CAUTION

Prodigal is followed by *of*, as in "We have been most *prodigal* of our resources."

95. OBSOLETE

Silly once meant *happy;* it derived from the German *saelig*, which in that language still means happy. But today no one uses *silly* in its old meaning—its original significance has gone completely out of use. The word's early meaning is *obsolete*.

In nature there are many *obsolete* forms—the dodo, the dinosaur, etc. Anything is *obsolete* which once was, but is no longer. We may speak of *obsolete* virtues, concepts, attitudes, words, meanings, pronunciations, fashions. Anything, too, which was once in general use, but has been discarded for more advanced forms, is *obsolete*, as certain kinds of war materials, types of automobiles or buildings, aircraft, engine designs, sailing vessels, hitching posts, coal cook-stoves, and so on.

DEFINITION

Obsolete means: no longer in use or existence.

PRONUNCIATIONS

Obsolete	ob'-sə-LEET'
Obsoleteness	OB'-sə-leet'-nəs

DERIVATION

Latin, *obsoletus*, worn out, fallen into disuse.

Test Your Learning

I. TRUE OR FALSE?

1. Society frowns upon *illicit* relationships.	True	False
2. *Licentious* books used to be banned in Boston.	True	False
3. Most men have *prodigious strength*.	True	False
4. *Prodigal* living cannot go on forever.	True	False
5. *Obsolete* words are in general use.	True	False

II. SAME OR OPPOSITE?

1. Illicit—unlawful	Same	Opposite
2. Licentious—lewd	Same	Opposite
3. Prodigious—customary	Same	Opposite
4. Prodigal—frugal	Same	Opposite
5. Obsolete—modern	Same	Opposite

III. USE THE WORD

1. For years he had maintained a (an) _____ relationship with his boss's wife.

2. Within a few years after a war, much of the armament becomes
_____.

3. He inherited a huge fortune, but _____ living soon reduced him to destitution.

4. Inhabitants of Greenwich Village have often been accused, perhaps unfairly, of _____ behavior.

5. Within one week he suffered the most _____ reverses; once a wealthy man, he was now practically a pauper.

IV. **WRITE THE WORD**
1. Discarded, out of use
2. Extraordinary in degree, extent, etc.
3. Unlawful and improper
4. Loose, uncontrolled, lewd
5. Extravagantly wasteful

1. _____
2. _____
3. _____
4. _____
5. _____

Check Your Learning

ANSWERS TO TESTS ON UNIT 18

TEST I
1—true, 2—true, 3—false, 4—true, 5—false.

TEST II
1—same, 2—same, 3—opposite, 4—opposite, 5—opposite.

TEST III
1—illicit, 2—obsolete, 3—prodigal, 4—licentious, 5—prodigious.

TEST IV
1—obsolete, 2—prodigious, 3—illicit, 4—licentious, 5—prodigal.

Unit Nineteen

96. SACRILEGIOUS

Certain things in life are considered sacred, though of course you would never get the iconoclast to agree to this philosophy. Largely venerated are the objects and rituals of religion, less commonly the privileges of position, power, wealth, and parenthood.

Obviously, one who steals sacred objects from a church or other house of worship is doing something wicked and profane. In Latin, the root *sacer* means *sacred*, the root *legere* means *to gather, pick up, take away, steal*—so a picker-up or thief of sacred objects was a *sacrilegus*, and, in English, a *sacrilegious* act is one which violates something sacred.

Sacrilege, the noun form, was originally restricted to profane and impious crimes against religion or religious precepts; today the word has an extended and more general meaning, and may refer also to any outrageous or wanton violation of the so-called sacred privileges accorded to position, power, wealth, parenthood, etc.

However, be cautious in using the word *sacrilegious* in a non-religious sense. If you and your family have been looking forward all week to the Sunday cut of prime ribs of beef that you have carefully saved your pennies for, and if, being a poor and careless cook, you ruin the beef by overroasting it, you may say, correctly and appropriately, as you gaze unhappily at the charred remains of a potentially succulent dinner, "Ah—it was a *sacrilege* to ruin that good beef!"

What you are doing, when you so use the word, is to ascribe, for purposes of obvious poetic exaggeration, sacred qualities to a cut of beef generally possessed only by true objects of worship and veneration. You are purposely exaggerating as the best means of expressing your deep feelings of hurt and regret.

People worship, in a sense, many things that are not of religious connection. Morton Thompson, in his exciting biography of Dr. Semmelweis, the discoverer of the causes of childbed fever,* describes how Dr. Jacob Klein, director of the Lying-in Division of the Vienna General

The Cry and the Covenant

Hospital, insisted that the beds in the obstetric ward be exactly equidistant one from the other. This was (to him) of crucial importance; for any bed to be out of line so much as an inch was a more heinous crime, was a greater act of wickedness, than that one out of five new mothers needlessly died of childbed fever. Hence, to move a bed from the exact position where it was designed to be was an act of *sacrilege,* a *sacrilegious* thing—again using the word, as in the case of the roast of beef, for purposes of poetic exaggeration.

In the same sense, to a die-hard reactionary, anything new and progressive is *sacrilegious;* to a firm, intransigent believer in parental authority, any childhood disobedience is *sacrilegious;* to a worshiper of wealth and power, any contemptuous reference to moneyed people is *sacrilegious.*

DEFINITION

Sacrilegious means: violating or profaning anything held sacred.

PRONUNCIATIONS

Sacrilegious   SAK′-rə-lee′-jəs *or* sak′-rə-LIJ′-əs
Sacrilege   SAK-rə-ləj

DERIVATION

Latin *sacer,* sacred, plus *legere* to steal, take away.

SPELLING CAUTION

Note that *sacrilegious* is spelled with the first two vowels in reverse order to that of *religious.* Let the derivation help you remember that the first vowel is *i,* the second *e; sacrilegious* starts with the first two syllables of *sacrifice* (which comes from the same root *sacer,* sacred), plus *leg* from *legere,* to steal.

97. RESONANT

It's all a matter of vibrations. In music, a tone can be enriched and intensified by supplementary vibrations, and singers who can conquer this technique have *resonance* and are, therefore, pleasant to listen to.

Resonance is from the Latin noun *sonus,* sound, plus the prefix *re,* again. A *resonant* tone resounds by means of supplementary vibrations, and is richer and more musical than, say, a squeak.

So a *resonant* tone is resounding, deep, full, rich, ringing. Caruso's *resonant* voice was a delight to hear, a church bell can peal *resonantly* throughout the village, the *resonant* qualities of William Jennings Bryan's voice explain, in part, why he was called the silver-tongued orator.

Resonance, then, is the prolongation of sound by reflection and re-verberation. A *resonant* tone is one that is amplified by the bones of the skull and upper chest and by the air cavities of the pharynx, mouth, and nasal passages. *Resonance* is usually a technique that has to be learned, practiced, and mastered by beginning singers and public speakers, and one of the common criticisms that a voice teacher finds with poor speakers is that they have not developed the ability to give *resonance* to their sounds.

DEFINITION

Resonant means: increasing the depth, richness, and intensity of sound
by means of supplementary vibrations.

PRONUNCIATIONS

Resonant	REZ'-ə-nənt
Resonance	REZ'-ə-nəns
Resonantly	REZ'-ə-nənt-lee

DERIVATION

Latin *sonus*, sound, plus *re*, again.

98. DISSONANT

Resonance may make a single sound deep and rich and beautiful, but when sounds are to be combined, as they are in music, there must also be harmony and compatibility—if sounds clash and conflict, the beauty is gone, all that is left is *dissonance*. Like *resonance*, *dissonance* also comes from the Latin *sonus*, sound, plus, in this instance, the prefix *dis*, away from. *Dissonant* chords, by derivation, sound away from, or in conflict with, each other; they are harsh, unmusical, discordant, unmelodious, unrestful. (Much of modern music is built on *dissonance*, and to the trained ear *dissonant* tones are not necessarily displeasing or unbeautiful, say the devotees of modern music.)

Dissonant may be used in a general sense, and need not be restricted exclusively to sound. We may speak of a man's statements as being *dissonant* from the truth, that is, incompatible with truth, disagreeing with facts; or we may say that a young girl's shy and recessive manner are strangely in *dissonance* with her sophisticated dress and appearance. Any things or actions which are in striking variance, which do not seem to go together, may be called *dissonant*.

DEFINITION

Dissonant means: disagreeing or harsh in sound; incompatible; not suitable one to the other.

PRONUNCIATIONS

Dissonant	DIS′-ə-nənt
Dissonance	DIS′-ə-nəns
Dissonantly	DIS′-ə-nənt-lee

DERIVATION

Latin *sonus,* sound, plus *dis,* away from.

99. UNISON

The root *sonus,* sound, is also found in the useful English word *unison,* which uses the Latin number *unus,* one, as a prefix. By derivation, then, *unison* is one sound.

When people answer in *unison,* they make, as it were, one sound; that is, they all speak at one time. If people sing in *unison,* they sing as if with one voice, in perfect harmony, all together, everyone always at the same word and pitch.

But again, as in the case of *dissonant,* the word need not be restricted to sound. People may act in *unison* (that is, cooperatively, together, working toward the same goal, in accord and harmony), work in *unison,* feel in *unison* about something (that is, have the same opinion), etc.

DEFINITION

Unison means: harmony, accord; making the same sound at the same time.

PRONUNCIATION

Unison   YOO′-nə-sən

Latin *sonus*, sound, plus *unus*, one.

100. DESULTORY

Sultum is from a Latin verb meaning *to jump*. *Insult* a person and, by derivation, you jump on him; *exult* over a triumph and, again by derivation, you jump out of yourself with joy; do something in a *desultory* fashion and you jump around aimlessly.

There is a great reverence among humanity for order, purpose, design. To have a predetermined goal in mind, to work methodically toward that goal, to finally reach it, this seems to give warmth, security, and direction to a person's life. So *desultoriness* is not a quality commonly held in high esteem.

How often have you heard people complain, "My reading has been very *desultory;* I should read with a purpose." (They may not have used this terminology, but the sentiment was the same.) They mean that their reading has been random, haphazard, with no continuity or direction; a mystery this week, a biography last week, a romantic novel before that.

People are unhappy when they lead a *desultory* life, when they live *desultorily*. If they change from one job to another, if they skip around from one activity to the next, if no method or system governs their actions, they lose their feeling of belonging, a feeling of utmost importance to the human organism.

Of course you may say that there is too much order and system in life, and we are therefore in danger of losing our spontaneity. That may well be. But little is accomplished if things are done in a *desultory* fashion, and a sense of accomplishment seems vital to many people.

If, for example, an author works on his book in a *desultory* fashion, he comes to it whenever the mood happens to seize him (which, in the case of most writers, is almost never); does a few paragraphs of one chapter, jumps around and writes a line or two of another chapter, a word here, a word or two there—and the result? The book never gets written.

Desultory means: aimless, governed by no purpose, goal, or system.

PRONUNCIATIONS

Desultory	DES′-əl-tawr′-ee
Desultoriness	DES′-əl-tawr′-ee-nəs
Desultorily	DES′-əl-tawr′-ə-lee

DERIVATION

Latin *sultum,* jump, plus *de,* around.

Test Your Learning

I. TRUE OR FALSE?

1. Iconoclasts are not reluctant to commit *sacrilegious* acts.   True   False
2. A *resonant* voice is rich and beautiful.   True   False
3. *Dissonance* is restful.   True   False
4. People who act in *unison* generally cooperate.   True   False
5. *Desultory* work goes on according to systematic plan.   True   False

II. SAME OR OPPOSITE?

1. Sacrilegious—impious   Same   Opposite
2. Resonant—deep   Same   Opposite
3. Dissonant—melodious   Same   Opposite
4. Unison—conflict   Same   Opposite
5. Desultory—aimless   Same   Opposite

III. USE THE WORD

1. The music of Stravinsky, one of the most famous of modern composers, is full of _____.
2. He spent the warm spring day in _____ wandering among the city's streets.
3. The teacher asked a question, and in _____ the students chorused an answer.
4. Few singers have the _____ quality of Caruso's rich voice.
5. In totalitarian countries, it is considered practically _____ to question the decisions of the leaders.

IV. WRITE THE WORD

1. A violation of sacred privilege or function   1. _____
2. With no goal or purpose   2. _____
3. Conflicting in sound, appearance, etc.   3. _____

4. Deep, rich, reverberating   4. _____

5. One voice; cooperation   5. _____

Check Your Learning

ANSWERS TO TESTS ON UNIT 19

TEST I

1—true, 2—true, 3—false, 4—true, 5—false.

TEST II

1—same, 2—same, 3—opposite, 4—opposite, 5—same.

TEST III

1—dissonance, 2—desultory, 3—unison, 4—resonant, 5—sacrilegious.

TEST IV

1—sacrilege, 2—desultory, 3—dissonant, 4—resonant, 5—unison.

Unit Twenty

101. AUSPICIOUS

Avis is the Latin root for *bird*, found, for example, in the English words *aviator* (one who flies like a bird) and *aviary* (a place or haven for birds).

Spicere or *specere* is the Latin root *to look* or *see*, found in such common English words as *inspect* (look into), *spectator* (a see-er or looker), *spectacle* (something worth seeing), *conspicuous* (easily seen), etc.

As you may know, U and V were two forms of the same letter in Latin, and so an *avispicum* or *auspicium* was, literally, a *bird watcher*. And why were birds watched so carefully in ancient Roman times?

Notice how the late Dr. Wilfred Funk explained it in his book, *Word Origins and Their Romantic Histories:*

> "The ancient priest and soothsayer watched the flight and feeding of birds, listened to their singing and their cries, and even examined their entrails, so that he could learn the wishes of the gods and so predict the future. If the signs came out well, the occasion was *auspicious,* or "of good omen." The derivation of this word illustrates the story as it is from the Latin term *auspicium,* formed of *avis*, "bird," and *specio*, "see." So these old diviners were really "bird watchers."

The term *auspicious,* then, may be applied to anything that is marked by favorable signs or circumstances, signs or circumstances which promise success or good results for the future.

Let us say that you start a new venture, the manufacture of a special type of lampshade. Your salesman calls first on Macy's in New York, and the buyer is so delighted with what he has to offer that she places an immediate order for five thousand shades. That, you will admit, is a most *auspicious* beginning, a sign that your venture will probably be a whopping success. Your new business has started most *auspiciously.*

Or let us say that an attorney passes his bar examination, is licensed and opens his law office. The first case that comes to him is a simple one, one he feels sure to win. He argues brilliantly in court, the evidence is all on his client's side—but the jury renders an adverse decision. That, fears the young lawyer, is a most *inauspicious* way to start his career—a way that makes him doubtful of his future.

"Let us wait for a more *auspicious* moment," someone suggests to you. He means that circumstances at this time do not seem favorable to success—he counsels waiting until the signs look better.

During an election, the first returns that come in are from a county that seemed highly doubtful. Yet your candidate has taken this county by a comfortable margin. This is not only good news, but *auspicious* also, for it is an indication of probable success in the entire election.

In short, something *auspicious* is not only good in itself, but a promise of even better things to come.

DEFINITION

Auspicious means: of good omen; betokening success; favorable.

PRONUNCIATIONS

Auspicious	aw-SPISH'-əs
Inauspicious	in'-aw-SPISH'-əs
Auspiciously	aw-SPISH'-əs-lee
Inauspiciously	in-aw-SPISH'-əs-lee

DERIVATION

Latin *auspicium*, a bird watcher.

102. PRECARIOUS

Precis is the Latin for prayer, and the English word *precarious*, by derivation, means obtained by begging or prayer.

Look at it this way. Get something by praying for it, rather than by deserving it, paying for it, or working for it, and you are depending on the whim and good will of the person who grants what you want. Under such circumstances, how can you be sure that by the same whim you won't suddenly and unexpectedly lose what you've got?

Anything *precarious*, then, is undependable, insecure, risky, unprotected. Writing, for example, is a *precarious* business: There is no cer-

THE ELLIOTT BAY BOOK COMPANY

244 .13   JAN 12, 1991 13:55:42

ISBN 0312043996 $ 8.95
ISBN 0399514007 $ 7.95
ISBN 1555363903 $ 14.95
            TOTAL $ 31.85
            TOTAL TAXABLE $ 31.85
            SALES TAX $ 2.61
            TOTAL DUE $ 34.46
CASH

   TOP OF THE RAIN...SNOW...ICE...
      January Readings at
    THE ELLIOTT BAY BOOK COMPANY

   David Jenkins   [Jan 2]
   Kenneth & Yarima Good 4:30 [Jan9]
   Children's Storytime 11 am [Jan5]
   Greg Child   [Jan 14]
   Robert Moore   [Jan 15]
   Michael Cunningham 5pm [Jan 16]
   Christopher Lasch 7:30 [Jan 16]
   walter Kirn   [Jan 17]
   Barbara Quick   [Jan 22]
   Martha Avery w/Zhang Xianliang
                        [Jan 23]
   (See our Store Readings Flyer)
   OPEN LATE DAILY: 10 AM - 11 PM
   M-SAT & 12-6 SUN & MOST HOLIDAYS
   Save this receipt for returns:
   refunds - 2 wks; exchanges-1 month

tainty of continuing success. The shifting interests of the public, a change in editors or editorial policy, can suddenly make an author's market disappear overnight. A civil service worker, on the other hand, has the least *precarious* of jobs—so long as he behaves himself morally and does his work efficiently, his employment and salary are likely to be secure. Political appointees, on the other hand, hold *precarious* tenure of office—a new administration or new director and they may again be unemployed.

Precarious does not necessarily mean dangerous, but rather insecure, undependable. The mountain climber who gets a *precarious* footing on a rock ledge is, of course, in danger of slipping, but it is the insecurity, not the danger, which is stressed when the footing is called *precarious*.

Coal mining and deep-sea diving are notoriously dangerous occupations, since physical danger is always present and must adequately be guarded against. But if the miners and divers can rely on steady employment and dependable wages, these occupations may not be labeled *precarious*.

A person, similarly, who is in *precarious* health is not necessarily sickly—he may be quite well, but such is his medical history that it is uncertain how long he will remain well, and tomorrow may see him bedridden. Note the stress on insecurity and uncertainty.

In a sense, of course, all life is *precarious*. There is always the chance of catastrophe, physical, economic, or political. Consolation may be taken however from the fact that 200 years ago the *precariousness* of life was considerably greater. The average person then was at the mercy of diseases that have now been conquered, was powerless against the caprice of government officials (his protection now lies in the modern concept of law and justice), had no certainty that a whim of his superior could not remove the props from his economic existence (labor unions, unemployment insurance, etc., protect him today). Life and sustenance in general became considerably less *precarious* (i.e. less dependent on the caprice of nature) as soon as man learned how to store and preserve food, and a bad crop no longer means mass famine, at least not in the more progressive countries of the world.

Thieves, confidence men, and bandits still live most *precariously*, but it is a manner of life they seem to prefer.

DEFINITION

Precarious means: dependent on circumstances beyond one's control; uncertain; insecure.

Precarious   prə-KAIR'-ee-əs
Precariously   prə-KAIR'-ee-əs-lee
Precariousness   prə-KAIR'-ee-əs-nəs

DERIVATION

Latin, *precarius*, obtained by prayer.

103. SPURIOUS

Take a counterfeit dollar bill. It makes every pretense of being genuine, imitating the color, design, and shape of true money, but once it is detected it is utterly worthless. It is, in a single word, *spurious*.

When a wealthy man dies intestate (that is, without leaving a will) and without close relatives, many people offer documents to prove that they were in some way related to the deceased, by blood or marriage or adoption. It is then the duty of the authorities to determine the genuineness of these documents, to use such scientific tests as will discover whether they are indeed what they are reputed to be. A birth certificate can be forged, a marriage license may have been altered, the handwriting that is claimed to be the deceased's may not be his at all. Any documents which cannot withstand such scientific analysis may be proved to be *spurious*.

Anything is *spurious*, then, which is claimed to be genuine, true, authentic, the real McCoy, but which is actually false, counterfeit, untrue, not genuine. There can be *spurious* statements, *spurious* money, *spurious* grief, *spurious* signatures, *spurious* first editions, *spurious* Rembrandts, etc. Something *spurious* is not what it pretends to be.

A person may contend *spuriously* that he is the illegitimate son of a king in order to be next in line for the throne; we say "*spuriously*" if we believe his contention false and intended to deceive. When taxed with the falsity of his claim, he may admit its *spuriousness*.

DEFINITION

Spurious means: not genuine or true; intended to deceive.

PRONUNCIATIONS

Spurious   SPYŌŌR'-ee-əs

| Spuriously | SPYŌŌR'-ee-əs-lee |
| Spuriousness | SPYŌŌR'-ee-əs-nəs |

DERIVATION

Latin *spurius*, false.

104. DILATORY

There are those who are the personification of promptness. If a piece of work is due by twelve noon on Monday, on Monday at noon it is in. If they promise that they will undertake a task, you may rely on it that they will get down to business expeditiously, they will not procrastinate, they will not waste time in dawdling.

Not everyone is so prompt and reliable, alas! A person can be most *dilatory* in answering his correspondence—a reply may not be forthcoming for weeks or months. A child may adopt a *dilatory* attitude toward those duties required by parents, but which he is most reluctant to get to, play and companionship with other children proving severe temptations toward delay and procrastination.

A commission may be appointed to investigate gambling. If the members of the commission are indifferent to the evils of gambling, they will be slow to begin investigating, it will take them a long time, perhaps by design, to get started. In a word, they will be serving their function *dilatorily*, or employing *dilatory* tactics.

A person, too, can be *dilatory* if he is in the habit of delaying things which he is responsible for doing promptly; if he is a procrastinator; if he is habitually slow in performing acts which should be performed on time; if he is customarily indifferent to the demands of time.

Call a person, an attitude, a tactic, etc., *dilatory* and you imply that the person responsible for prompt performance is either purposely going slow for ulterior and hidden purposes of his own, or because he is indifferent to the need for quick action.

DEFINITION

Dilatory means: slow, delaying, procrastinating because of neglect or indifference.

PRONUNCIATIONS

| Dilatory | DIL'-ə-taw'-ree |

Dilatorily	DIL'-ə-TAW'-rə-lee
Dilatoriness	DIL'-ə-taw'-ree-nəs

DERIVATION

Latin, *dilatus*, delayed.

105. INCONGRUOUS

Consider dress. Would you wear a pair of riding boots with a tuxedo? A pair of rubber boots or bedroom slippers with an evening gown? Would you attend college commencement exercises in slacks and a polo shirt, or a formal wedding in a halter and shorts?

Consider language. Would you expect to hear blasphemy and vulgarity from a church pulpit? Or words like "divine," "cute," "adorable," "precious" from a stevedore or coal miner or truck driver? Or grossly illiterate grammar from a college professor?

Consider furnishings. Do you find richly brocaded tapestries and thick carpets in a summer cottage on the beach? Broken-down wood chairs and orange boxes for tables in the living room of a Fifth Avenue (New York, that is) mansion?

Consider, finally, actions and motives. Do you normally find a young child always selfless, always completely considerate of others? A militant labor leader on the side of the reactionary capitalists? A high military officer ardently expounding pacifism, demobilization, unpreparedness? A person of vast and inherited wealth carefully hoarding his pennies, denying himself little luxuries so he can save money, living frugally, keeping strictly to a low budget?

The single, uniform answer to these similar questions is of course No. In normal human living certain things suitably, properly, and fittingly go together, like ham and eggs, apple pie and cheese, roast beef and Yorkshire pudding. Those things which are completely out of place with their surroundings, actual or figurative, are *incongruous*. A pair of riding boots is *incongruous* at a formal affair, as is a halter or a polo shirt. Coarse language from the pulpit, affected words on the tongue of a dock laborer, bad grammar from a person of education are, in the same way, *incongruous*.

Motives inconsistent with wealth are an *incongruity* in a wealthy person, poor furnishings are *incongruities* in a mansion.

Whatever, then, is out of place, unfitting, improper, unsuitable, in clashing contrast with its surroundings, in striking conflict with the general picture, may be called *incongruous*, or is an *incongruity*.

"It's so *incongruous* to hear you worrying about whether you made a good impression, when I know you don't give a rap for what people think of you," someone may say, expressing surprise at a form of behavior which is unexpectedly inconsistent with your general pattern of conduct.

"Your little house looks so *incongruous* in that neighborhood of sprawling estates and huge mansions," someone else may say, again referring to the surprising contrast between something and its surroundings.

To sum it up briefly, something is *incongruous* if it just doesn't seem to belong.

DEFINITION

Incongruous means: out of keeping, inappropriate, inconsistent, out of place in its surroundings.

PRONUNCIATIONS

Incongruous	in-KONG'-gr$\overline{oo}$-əs
Incongruity	in'-kəng-GR$\overline{OO}$'-ə-tee

DERIVATION

Latin *congruous*, fit, agreeing, plus *in*, not.

Test Your Learning

I. TRUE OR FALSE?

1. If something begins *auspiciously*, success is more likely than if it begins *inauspiciously*.   *True   False*
2. A *precarious* livelihood is uncertain and insecure.   *True   False*
3. A *spurious* bill is counterfeit.   *True   False*
4. A *dilatory* attitude is characteristic of prompt people.   *True   False*
5. Life is full of *incongruities*.   *True   False*

II. SAME OR OPPOSITE?

1. Auspicious—favorable   *Same   Opposite*
2. Precarious—dependable   *Same   Opposite*
3. Spurious—genuine   *Same   Opposite*
4. Dilatory—delaying   *Same   Opposite*
5. Incongruous—inconsistent   *Same   Opposite*

153

III. USE THE WORD

1. He was scrambling _____ly up the mountain ledge, at every step seemingly on the verge of losing his footing.
2. His career, while finally prodigiously successful, started, oddly enough, most _____ly.
3. The commission, which kept asking for more and more time, was accused of all manner of _____ tactics.
4. It is so _____ for Richard, who is six feet four, to have married Muriel, who is four feet eight.
5. When his claim was proved _____, the case was thrown out of court.

IV. WRITE THE WORD

1. Insecure, undependable   1. _____
2. Out of place, inconsistent   2. _____
3. Not genuine   3. _____
4. Favorable, promising future success   4. _____
5. Delaying, procrastinating, slow   5. _____

Check Your Learning

ANSWERS TO TESTS ON UNIT 20

TEST I

1—true, 2—true, 3—true, 4—false, 5—true.

TEST II

1—same, 2—opposite, 3—opposite, 4—same, 5—same.

TEST III

1—precarious, 2—inauspicious, 3—dilatory, 4—incongruous, 5—spurious.

TEST IV

1—precarious, 2—incongruous, 3—spurious, 4—auspicious, 5—dilatory.

Review Test V

(A complete Check on Your Understanding of Words 86–105)

I. SAME OR OPPOSITE?

1. Perfunctory—indifferent	Same	Opposite
2. Facetious—serious	Same	Opposite
3. Veracious—truthful	Same	Opposite
4. Mendacious—deceptive	Same	Opposite
5. Wanton—uncontrolled	Same	Opposite

6. Illicit—illegal   *Same*   *Opposite*
7. Licentious—restrained   *Same*   *Opposite*
8. Prodigious—unusual   *Same*   *Opposite*
9. Prodigal—frugal   *Same*   *Opposite*
10. Obsolete—modern   *Same*   *Opposite*
11. Sacrilegious—reverential   *Same*   *Opposite*
12. Resonant—squeaky   *Same*   *Opposite*
13. Dissonant—harmonious   *Same*   *Opposite*
14. Unison—conflict   *Same*   *Opposite*
15. Desultory—aimless   *Same*   *Opposite*
16. Auspicious—favorable   *Same*   *Opposite*
17. Precarious—insecure   *Same*   *Opposite*
18. Spurious—authentic   *Same*   *Opposite*
19. Dilatory—prompt   *Same*   *Opposite*
20. Incongruous—unsuitable   *Same*   *Opposite*

II. FORMING NOUNS

Change each adjective to its corresponding noun which will fit into the accompanying phrase. Avoid the ending "*ness*."

1. Veracious—noted for his _____.
2. Mendacious—condemned for his _____.
3. Prodigal—his habit of _____.
4. Sacrilegious—a contemptible _____.
5. Resonant—insufficient _____.
6. Dissonant—built on _____.
7. Incongruous—a surprising _____.

III. MATCHING A

I	II
1. perfunctory	a—irreverent
2. illicit	b—unsuitable
3. sacrilegious	c—favorable
4. auspicious	d—uninspired
5. incongruous	e—illegal

IV. MATCHING B

I	II
1. facetious	a—sexually depraved
2. licentious	b—deep, reverberating
3. resonant	c—humorous

4. precarious   d—aimless

5. desultory   e—insecure

V. MATCHING C

I	II
1. veracious	a—clashing
2. prodigious	b—discarded
3. dissonant	c—false
4. spurious	d—truthful
5. obsolete	e—phenomenal

VI. MATCHING D

I	II
1. mendacious	a—wasteful
2. prodigal	b—delaying
3. in unison	c—untruthful
4. dilatory	d—simultaneously
5. wanton	e—unprovoked

Check Your Learning

ANSWERS TO REVIEW TEST V

TEST I

1—same, 2—opposite, 3—same, 4—same, 5—same, 6—same, 7—opposite, 8—same, 9—opposite, 10—opposite, 11—opposite, 12—opposite, 13—opposite, 14—opposite, 15—same, 16—same, 17—same, 18—opposite, 19—opposite, 20—same.

TEST II

1—veracity, 2—mendacity, 3—prodigality, 4—sacrilege, 5—resonance, 6—dissonance, 7—incongruity.

TEST III

1—d, 2—e, 3—a, 4—c, 5—b.

TEST IV

1—c, 2—a, 3—b, 4—e, 5—d.

TEST V

1—d, 2—e, 3—a, 4—c, 5—b.

TEST VI

1—c, 2—a, 3—d, 4—b, 5—e.

PART VI

The Law

We discuss, in this final Part, 25 common legal terms that are frequently found in print and often heard in conversation, but which may be most confusing to the average person.

Do you know, for example, the distinction between:

A felony and a misdemeanor?
Homicide, murder, and manslaughter?
Burglary and robbery?
Rape, adultery, seduction, and incest?
Forgery and perjury?
A commutation, a parole, and a pardon?
Mayhem and assault?

Read on . . .

Unit Twenty-One

106. ARSON

The discovery of fire, in some remote prehistoric day, was one of the first steps in man's great advance over the animals. (It is on a par with his invention of the wheel and with his use of intelligible sounds, instead of mere gestures, for the purpose of communication.)

You would be hard put to it, today, to think of life without fire. We cook with it, heat our homes, generate electrical power, make steel and plastics and chemicals, and warm the baby's bottle. With fire in one form or another, we run cars, airplanes, and trains.

Fire, our greatest industrial agent, is at times our greatest foe. We lose thousands of acres of timberland, hundreds of lives, millions of dollars worth of property every year through uncontrolled fire. So fire may be a weapon for evil and destruction, as well as for good, and there are people in the world who use it for criminal purposes. Maliciously and wilfully they set fire to their neighbors' homes or other buildings, or to their own homes or property for the purpose of collecting insurance. They are then guilty of *arson*, and when apprehended and convicted, may be punished by jail sentences.

Fire which results in the destruction of life or property is not necessarily *arson*—certainly not if the fire occurred accidentally or through negligence. *Arson* implies malice and deliberate purpose; commonly, the motive of the *arsonist* is economic gain, through the collection of an insurance policy, although his action may spring also from a desire for revenge or simple maliciousness.

DEFINITION

Arson: the illegal burning of property, one's own or another's, wilfully, maliciously, or for purposes of fraud.

PRONUNCIATIONS

Arson   AHR'-sən
Arsonist   AHR'-sən-ist

Latin, *arsum*, to burn.

107. FELONY

Arson is a *felony*, that is, one of the more serious types of crimes. In most states, forgery, bribery, perjury,* theft, fraudulent bankruptcy, bigamy,* rape,* burglary,* kidnaping and murder* are among the crimes considered *felonious*. The penalty for any *felony* in many jurisdictions is a year or more imprisonment, and the convicted *felon* in addition suffers loss of his civil rights: he cannot vote, hold office, obtain a gun permit, become a doctor, lawyer, certified public accountant, chiropodist, notary public, dentist, etc., or if he already pursues such or similar professions, his license to continue doing so is revoked. Committing a *felony* is, as you see, a grave offense against society—and being caught and convicted is no laughing matter.

DEFINITION

Felony: a serious criminal offense.

PRONUNCIATIONS

Felony	FEL'-ə-nee
Felonious	fə-LŌ-nee-əs
Felon	FEL'-ən

DERIVATION

Latin *fel*, gall, nerve, used in middle English as an adjective meaning cruel or as a noun meaning villain.

108. MISDEMEANOR

An offense against society which is less serious than a felony is termed, in law, a *misdemeanor*. The distinction between felonies and *misdemeanors* is arbitrary, and may possibly vary from state to state, but many classify any violation of law that receives less than one year's

*Those crimes are discussed in detail in this or later units of Part VI.

imprisonment as punishment as a *misdemeanor*. Park illegally; exceed the speed limit; throw garbage out of your car as you cruise the countryside; smoke in a street-car or bus; and you may be guilty of a *misdemeanor*. If you are caught and convicted, you may be fined, or imprisoned for no more than a year, and your civil rights may not be taken away from you. Some more recent criminal codes do not distinguish between misdemeanors and felonies; instead, they classify crimes according to their degree of seriousness.

DEFINITION

Misdemeanor: a less serious offense than a felony.

PRONUNCIATION

Misdemeanor   mis'-də-MEE'-nər

DERIVATION

Latin *demener*, conduct oneself, plus the prefix *mis, wrongly*.

USAGE CAUTION

With both *felony* and *misdemeanor* the commonly used verb is *commit* or *be guilty of*. Occasionally with *felony, perpetrate* is also used. Note the following patterns.

He was accused of perpetrating a *felony*.

He committed a *misdemeanor*.

He was judged guilty of a *misdemeanor*.

Anyone smoking in the subways in New York City is committing a *misdemeanor*.

109. BIGAMY

Few sane people would knowingly marry a second spouse while still legally wed to the first one, and simultaneously having two or more spouses to support financially and cater to emotionally should itself be punishment enough, and usually is; but the law often steps in to protect those who are not sufficiently sane or strong-willed to protect themselves, and *bigamy*, the contraction of a marriage while a previous marriage is still legally in force, is not only a crime but, in some places, also a felony. Both men and women may be guilty of *bigamy*, though only that party to a *bigamous* marriage who has failed to dissolve his (or her) previous married state is guilty of the crime. Thus, if Doris, who has a legal husband in Arizona, marries Sam, who has not previously been married (or whose previous wife has died or has legally divorced him), only Doris is a *bigamist*—not Sam.

Needless to say, the children of a *bigamous* marriage are not recognized by law as legitimate offspring.

DEFINITION

Bigamy: the criminal offense of wilfully contracting a marriage while a previous marriage is, to the knowledge of the offender, still legally in force.

PRONUNCIATIONS

Bigamy	BIG'-ə-mee
Bigamous	BIG'-ə-məs
Bigamist	BIG'-ə-mist

DERIVATION

Greek *gamos,* marriage, plus *bi,* two.

110. PERJURY

As a price for living in society, there are, as you see, many things people may not do, on pain of punishment. They may not maliciously destroy property by fire (arson) or have more than one legal spouse (bigamy). Also, they may not knowingly tell a falsehood when they have taken an oath to tell the truth, or they have committed *perjury,* which, in most states, is a felony and punishable as such.

The crime of *perjury* is of course restricted to legal processes. If you swear to tell your spouse the truth about your whereabouts the night before and then lie convincingly through your teeth, you are not guilty of *perjury* unless this lie is perpetrated in a courtroom while you are under legal oath, or in some legal paper (affidavit, deposition, etc.) to which you have sworn. (When your lie is discovered you will be punished in a manner likely far worse than a sojourn in the county penitentiary.)

One can *perjure* oneself just as completely by making false statements in a legal paper or tax return as by distorting the truth while on the witness stand. And in most states of the union, the *perjurer* is not lightly dealt with.

And if you persuade or bribe someone else to lie while under oath, you are equally guilty; the crime is then called *subornation* (sub-awr-NAY'-shən) of *perjury*.

DEFINITION

Perjury: the crime of wilfully lying while under legal oath.

PRONUNCIATIONS

Perjury	PUR'-jə-ree
Perjurer	PUR'-jə-rər
To perjure	PUR'-jər

DERIVATION

Latin, *jurare,* to swear, take oath.

Test Your Learning

I. TRUE OR FALSE?

1. Someone who carelessly discards a lighted cigarette which causes a forest fire is guilty of *arson*. True False
2. A *felony* is a serious crime. True False
3. A *misdemeanor* is punished more seriously than a *felony*. True False
4. A man who marries a second time after legally divorcing his first wife is a *bigamist*. True False
5. Anyone who tells a lie is a *perjurer*. True False

II. MATCHING

From column II choose the activity that is related to each crime in column I.

I	II
1. arson	a—parking over time
2. felony	b—murder
3. misdemeanor	c—falsehood under oath
4. bigamy	d—setting fires maliciously
5. perjury	e—illegal second marriage

1. His testimony proved to us that he was willing to _____ himself.
2. In many localities, if you litter a public beach you are guilty of a _____.
3. He ran away from his wife in Connecticut and married an unsuspecting girl in Virginia; eventually he was apprehended and prosecuted for _____.
4. The insurance company refused to pay his claim, suspecting _____.
5. In this country, murder is one _____ sometimes punishable by death.

IV. WRITE THE WORD

1. A serious crime   1. _____
2. A less serious violation of law   2. _____
3. Illegal marrying of another while a previous marriage
   is in force   3. _____
4. False statements under legal oath   4. _____
5. Malicious setting fire to a home or structure   5. _____

Check Your Learning

ANSWERS TO TESTS ON UNIT 21

TEST I

   1—false, 2—true, 3—false, 4—false, 5—false.

TEST II

   1—d, 2—b, 3—a, 4—e, 5—c.

TEST III

   1—perjure, 2—misdemeanor, 3—bigamy, 4—arson, 5—felony.

TEST IV

   1—felony, 2—misdemeanor, 3—bigamy, 4—perjury, 5—arson.

Unit Twenty-Two

111. HOMICIDE

Society, then, places various restrictions on human conduct, usually enforcing these restrictions by legal means. Actions which threaten life, limb, property, the stability of family relations, etc., are termed crimes and are punishable by death, imprisonment, or financial penalties.

Extremely severe penalties are generally exacted for crimes against the person, and in some states of the union murder, for example, is punishable by some form of execution, commonly electrocution (capital punishment). Murder, in a sense, is the ultimate crime against society and usually faces the ultimate penalty, whether it be execution or life imprisonment.

Murder and *manslaughter*, which will be discussed in detail in later sections of this unit, are special forms of *homicide*, but *homicide* by itself is not a crime, referring, simply, to the killing of a human being. A distinction is usually made between *justifiable homicide, excusable homicide,* and *felonious homicide*.

If an officer of the law executes the death penalty upon a convicted murderer (as when the warden of a prison throws the switch that activates the electric chair), *justifiable homicide* is taking place, and obviously no crime is being committed. Similarly, when an officer kills someone as the only means of preventing him from committing a felony, that too is *justifiable homicide*.

If someone comes at you with a club, and you assume reasonably that he intends to bash your head in, no one will blame you for killing him in self-defense. Such an act on your part would be termed *excusable homicide*.

But if you wrongfully kill a human being, with no justification or excuse in law, you are committing *felonious homicide*, either *manslaughter* or *murder*, depending on the circumstances.

Homicide, then, is a neutral and general term, and is a felony only if the special circumstances to be described shortly are such as to render it either *manslaughter* or *murder*.

The adjective form of the word is *homicidal*—in certain types of insanity, for example, the victim has *homicidal* tendencies, that is, his mania is such as to render him likely to kill.

DEFINITION

Homicide: the killing of a human being.

PRONUNCIATIONS

Homicide	HOM'-ə-sīd'
Homicidal	hom'-ə-sīd'-əl

DERIVATION

Latin, *caedo,* to kill, plus *homo,* a human being.

112. MANSLAUGHTER

You are driving sixty miles an hour on a road posted for good reasons at twenty-five. It is a rainy, skiddy night. Suddenly you see a dog in your path. You slam on the brakes, your car goes into a tailspin skid, and you crash into a pedestrian innocently waiting on the corner for a street car. As luck would have it, you kill him instantly.

Notice the circumstances: You had no intent to end the pedestrian's life, it was the furthest thing from your mind, but his death resulted from your negligence and wilfulness in violating the traffic law that imposed a low rate of speed on a hazardous road.

You have committed *manslaughter.* You have killed a human being, though obviously without intent or malice. Concomitant with the killing, you were breaking the law, and it might be argued that if you had traveled at a more reasonable rate of speed the pedestrian would still be alive, for you would have had better control of your car. The fact remains, nevertheless, that not for one moment did you plan to kill the deceased, nor even do bodily harm of any sort to him.

That is one common type of *manslaughter.* Here is another.

It is the Fourth of July and like millions of other fun-loving Americans you are watching your money go up in smoke, as you set off firecrackers, light Roman Candles, twirl sparklers, etc. All this is socially acceptable and, in the locality in which you are celebrating, perfectly legal. Then you happen to see a group of your friends gathered around a bonfire, and the devil gets into you. You toss a string of harmless "salutes" into the fire, they go off with a few feeble pops and swishes, and an old man in the group falls dead—of heart failure. The sudden noise and the unexpected movement, combined with the excitement of the evening, were too much for his weak and aging organ. Again you have, technically, committed *manslaughter*, the wrongful killing of a human being, but without malice or intent. (Probably, in this instance, a jury would acquit you if you could establish that you had no knowledge or suspicion that the deceased suffered from heart trouble.)

Here are some further instances of *manslaughter*. Notice in each case the complete absence of an intent to kill.

1. You are a prizefighter and are taking part in a legal match. One of your blows, delivered to that part of your opponent's anatomy and in such a manner as are both completely lawful in boxing, knocks the opposing fighter unconscious. Shortly thereafter he dies, his death directly attributable to the injury caused by your blow.

2. You are lawfully hunting in the woods and take aim at what you believe is a quail but which, unfortunately for all concerned, turns out to be a fellow hunter. Your bullet goes cleanly through his skull and kills him.

3. You are carrying a hod of bricks up a ladder. On one of the upper rungs you miss your footing, several bricks plummet to the ground, and an unsuperstitious and hatless passerby walking under the ladder is neatly brained and immediately killed.

4. You are engaging in a furious argument with a friend and in exasperation you shove him slightly. As he falls back, he trips over a loose end of the rug and strikes his head so forcibly on the stone fireplace behind him that he sustains a brain injury from which he eventually dies.

In all these and any similar circumstances, you would be judged guilty of *manslaugher* rather than murder; the penalty, if any, would probably depend on the degree of negligence accompanying your actions.

DEFINITION

Manslaughter: the unlawful killing of a human being, whether voluntarily or involuntarily, but without previously expressed or implied malice, intent, purpose, deliberation, or premeditation.

PRONUNCIATION

Manslaughter   MAN'-slaw-tər

Combination of the English words *man* and *slaughter*.

113. MURDER

The essence of *murder* is that it is committed with malice aforethought, with deliberate planning and premeditation, and by a person who is judged legally sane and therefore is aware of the wrongness of his act. Furthermore, in most states, a killing or homicide is termed murder if it occurs during the commission of certain felonies, such as arson, rape, robbery, or burglary, even though the killer had no preconceived intent to commit murder.

In some states, lesser degrees of murder are defined. Consider the following circumstances:

You are shopping in a supermarket and someone, a perfect stranger, elbows his way past you to have his purchases checked by the cashier. You remonstrate forcibly, the other person answers in kind, and a violent argument ensues. You suddenly lose all control of yourself, pick up a pointed bill-holder from the counter and stab your opponent to death.

This type of killing would be called second degree murder in some states, but in other states, where the legal definition might vary, a killing in the heat of passion such as the one described in the supermarket incident might be termed manslaughter, and the penalty would depend on the statutes of the state in which the crime is committed.

DEFINITION

Murder is commonly understood to be the killing of a human being with purposeful deliberation, premeditation, malice aforethought.

PRONUNCIATIONS

Murder	MUR′-dər
Murderer	MUR′-dər-ər
Murderous	MUR′-dər-əs

DERIVATION

Anglo-Saxon *morthor,* murder.

114. BURGLARY

Burglary is, of course, a form of thievery, but has special characteristics not found, for example, in shoplifting, pilfering, swindling, embezzlement* or robbery.

The strict legal definition of *burglary* is theft from a premises committed after breaking and entering that premises, or breaking and entering a premises for the purpose of committing a theft or other felony.

Thus, if you have been invited for lunch to a friend's house, and you swipe a sterling silver shrimp fork when no one is looking, you have not committed *burglary*. Or if your friend falls asleep after a heavy meal and you lift his wallet, you are still not guilty of *burglary*.

But pick a lock and enter someone's house, vacant or occupied, for the purpose of stealing something in the house, and you have thereby become a *burglar*, irrespective of whether you actually take anything. (The professional *burglar* of course rarely comes away empty-handed.) Or gain illegal entrance into any sort of premises (store, office, shop, apartment, etc.) with the intent of acting feloniously and you may be accused of *burglarizing*. (This is the proper form of the verb; to *burgle* is not acceptable in educated usage.)

The important characteristic of *burglary*, then, as a type of thievery, the prerequisite element that distinguishes it from other forms, is *illegal and forcible entry*.

Note that "forcible entry" does not necessarily mean violent entry. You do not have to batter down a door or break a lock beyond all repair for the law to consider that you have gained forcible entry to a premises. If no more than a cloth curtain separates you from the inside of someone's house, and you push that curtain aside, however gently, to enter illegally and to steal whatever it is that you are after, you are guilty of *burglary*—you have used force, slight as it may have been. Or if a door is unlocked, or even ajar, any slight pushing of the door to gain entrance is "forcible" in the eyes of the law. On the other hand, if the door is wide open and you walk in to steal, your entry may have been illegal, but was not forcible. Force being completely absent, you have perhaps stolen, but have not, technically speaking, committed *burglary*. Or if you walk across someone's lawn and pick up a diamond brooch which the owner negligently left outside, again your thievery cannot legally be considered *burglary*.

*Discussed in Unit 23.

Burglary: forcible and illegal entry into a building for felonious purposes.

Burglary	BUR'-glə-ree
Burglarize	BUR'-glə-rīz
Burglar	BUR'-glər

Latin *burglator,* of similar meaning.

115. ROBBERY

Robbery, too, has its clear-cut and distinctive characteristics. Several elements must be present. To begin with, you must take something from a person, something either actually in his physical possession or in his presence, before you may be accused of *robbery.*

Second, the taking must be against the owner's will.

And third, the thievery must be committed by force or intimidation.

The obvious example of a *robber* (from the strictly legal standpoint) is the gangster who points a gun at you and threatens death or bodily harm if you do not forthwith deliver your wallet to him.

Note that all three elements of *robbery* are in effect. The wallet was on your person; you had no desire to be rid of it; and you acted under threats and fear.

A man who holds up an armored car at gunpoint is committing *robbery.* By means of intimidation he is stealing, in the presence of the guards entrusted with it and obviously against their will, money to which he has no legal right. (When a baseball fan yells "We wuz *robbed!*" he is using the word in its general, rather than legal, sense.)

Robbery: the felonious taking of personal property from someone, forcibly or by intimidation, and against his will.

PRONUNCIATIONS

Robbery   ROB'-ə-ree
Robber   ROB'-ər

DERIVATION

Old French *roberie,* of similar meaning.

Test Your Learning

I. TRUE OR FALSE?

1. All *homicide* is legally punishable.   True   False
2. *Manslaughter* is a deliberate, preconceived, and premeditated crime.   True   False
3. A killing which results during the commission of a felonious crime may be termed *murder.*   True   False
4. *Burglary* presupposes forcible and illegal entry.   True   False
5. Taking something from a department store without paying for it is *robbery.*   True   False

II. MATCHING

I	II
1. manslaughter	a—planning and executing an illegal killing
2. robbery	b—any act which deprives a human being of his life, justifiable or otherwise, accidental or designed
3. murder	
4. burglary	c—illegal killing of a human being without malice aforethought
5. homicide	
	d—illegal and forcible entry into a building for felonious purposes
	e—theft from a person by force or intimidation

III. WRITE THE WORD

1. Theft from a person   1. _____
2. Illegal killing without premeditation   2. _____
3. Illegal killing with deliberate planning and design   3. _____
4. Any killing of a human   4. _____
5. Theft after breaking and entering   5. _____

Check Your Learning

TEST I

1—false, 2—false, 3—true, 4—true, 5—false.

TEST II

1—c, 2—e, 3—a, 4—d, 5—b.

TEST III

1—robbery, 2—manslaughter, 3—murder, 4—homicide, 5—burglary.

Unit Twenty-Three

116. RAPE

In modern civilization, laws are designed to protect life, limb, property, and, in the case of three specific crimes to be discussed in this Unit, morals and chastity. From the earliest days of civilization, society has placed certain restrictions on sexual behavior and has severely penalized any flagrant rebellion against its control.

It is illegal in this country, as it is in most civilized regions of the world, for a man to force a woman who is not married to him to submit to intimate relations against her will; such action on a man's part is termed *rape* and variously punished in different states of the union by fine or imprisonment or both.

Since *rape* is in general difficult if not impossible to prove, there being few if any outside witnesses to the act, the laws of a state describe with great detail what shall or shall not constitute the crime. Usually if the female has not reached a specified chronological age (termed the "age of consent," which may vary from state to state), the man involved is automatically guilty of *rape* no matter how willing or even inviting his partner may have been. In most states, even attempted *rape* is a crime, no matter what the degree of success or failure. Traditionally, only a man, never a woman,* can be guilty of rape, can legally be termed a *rapist*. Today, however, some states have replaced their rape statutes with sexual assault laws that do not distinguish between men and women, and that apply to married couples as well as to unmarried people.

---

*Except under one interesting circumstance. If a woman helps a man *rape* another woman, she is considered equally guilty with him, for she is an accessory to his crime. She may help the *rapist* by holding the victim forcibly while the act is committed, or lure the victim into a deserted place under false pretenses, etc.

Rape: unlawful carnal knowledge of a woman by a man forcibly and
against her will; or such an act with a female below the "age of
consent."

PRONUNCIATIONS

Rape	RAYP
Rapist	RAY'-pist

DERIVATION

Latin *rapere,* to seize.

117. ADULTERY

It is likewise illegal for a married man or woman to have sexual relations
with a person other than his or her own spouse—the crime is *adultery*
and is punishable under law. The exact definition varies from state to
state; in some states (as under the old Roman and Jewish law) *adultery*
is committed only when the *woman* is married to a third person; in
most states, when *either party* is married. Under the laws of some states,
if one person is married and the other single, only the married person
is guilty of *adultery;* under the laws of other states, both parties have
committed *adultery*.

A person who has committed *adultery* is, if a man, an *adulterer;* if a
woman, an *adulteress*. In Hawthorne's *The Scarlet Letter,* Hester Prynne
was forced to wear the infamous "A" on her bosom because she was
deemed guilty of *adultery*—relations with a married man.

DEFINITION

Adultery: voluntary sexual relations of a married person with someone
other than his or her spouse.

PRONUNCIATIONS

Adultery	ə-DUL'-tə-ree
Adulterer	ə-DUL'-tə-rər
Adulteress	ə-DUL'-tə-rəs
Adulterous	ə-DUL'-tə-rəs

DERIVATION

Latin *adulterium,* of similar meaning. There is no close connection in
derivation between *adultery* and *adult*. *Adultery,* like *adulterate,*

comes ultimately from the Latin words *ad*, to, and *alter*, another. When you adulterate food, you make it into something other than what it was; when you commit adultery, you perform the act with another than the one with whom it is legally permissible. *Adult*, on the other hand, comes from one of the forms of the Latin verb *adolescere*, to grow up, as also does *adolescent*.

118. INCEST

The crime of *incest* is committed when the two parties to a sexual act are related to each other in the degree within which marriage is forbidden by law—mother and son, father and daughter, brother and sister, aunt and nephew, uncle and niece, etc. Desire of a daughter by her father, etc., is termed *incestuous*.

PRONUNCIATIONS

Incest	IN'-sest'
Incestuous	in-SES'-choo-əs
Incestuously	in-SES'-choo-əs-lee

DERIVATION

Latin *castus*, chaste, plus *in*, not.

119. EMBEZZLEMENT

A burglar, we have decided, gains forcible entry into a premises in order to steal someone's property; a robber through force or intimidation steals property from the person or within the presence of the owner. An *embezzler* is a much less fearsome character, though his thievery may be just as serious and inconveniencing as that of the burglar or robber. He does not pick locks or climb through windows, nor does he hold people up at gunpoint. Rather, he appropriates to his own use money or property that is lawfully in his possession, although he does not legally own it. And he does this without the consent or knowledge of the owner.

For example, a bank teller may become an *embezzler*. The money in the cash drawer is legally in his possession, since he obtained it by no force, ruse, or fraud, but in the regular course of the bank's business. However, it is not his money, it is not there for his use, and it is only temporarily entrusted to his care, his employers taking for granted that he is an honest man.

Perhaps he is an honest man—but the temptations of horse racing and expensive women may be too much for him and he decides to "borrow" whatever sums he needs to place a bet or take out a blonde. He may consider it "borrowing," but the law calls it *embezzlement*.

To *embezzle* is a crime, and most types of *embezzlement* are felonies, no matter how sincere the *embezzler* may have been in his intention to repay the money or restore the property he has fraudulently appropriated.

So any bank officer or employee, or the trustee of an estate, or a public officer, or the treasurer of a corporation, or in fact any person to whom money or property is legally entrusted may be guilty of *embezzlement* if he takes the money or property for his own use. Penalties for the crime vary with the type of *embezzlement* involved.

DEFINITION

Embezzlement: the fraudulent appropriation to one's own use of the money or property entrusted to one's care.

PRONUNCIATIONS

Embezzlement	əm-BEZ'-əl-mənt
Embezzle	əm-BEZ'-əl
Embezzler	əm-BEZ'-lər

DERIVATION

Old French, *embesillier*, of similar meaning.

120. FORGERY

Write out a check for any sum and sign not your own name but the name of a person who has funds in the bank on which the check is drawn; and do this with the intent to defraud the bank of money to which you have no legal right. You have, under these circumstances, committed *forgery*. (The bank may detect the fraud before turning any money over to you, you may not make a cent out of the deal, your efforts may be totally and embarrassingly unsuccessful; you are nevertheless guilty of the crime of *forgery*—it is the act and the intent which count, not the success or failure.)

Likewise, with the same fraudulent purpose, endorse a check or postal order with someone else's signature, or materially alter the writing of a will, check, or other legal document, and you are committing *forgery*.

The altered document itself, or the spurious signature, is also called a *forgery*.

DEFINITION

Forgery: crime of imitating the signature of another, or altering the writing of a legal document, for purposes of fraud.

PRONUNCIATIONS

Forgery	FAWR′-jə-ree
Forge	FAWRJ
Forger	FAWR′-jər

DERIVATION

Old French, *forgier*, to form or fashion.

Test Your Learning

I. TRUE OR FALSE?

1. Only a married man can commit *rape*.   True   False
2. Two unmarried people cannot commit *adultery*.   True   False
3. *Incestuous* acts are punishable by law.   True   False
4. An *embezzler* is a criminal.   True   False
5. Writing another person's name purely for amusement
   and with no intent to defraud is still *forgery*.   True   False

II. MATCHING

I	II
1. rape	a—illegal copying of another's signature for purposes of fraud
2. adultery	
3. incest	b—unlawful sexual relations when one of the partners is married to a third person
4. embezzlement	
5. forgery	c—illegal appropriation of funds entrusted to one's care

> d—sexual relations forced upon a woman
> against her will
> e—unlawful sexual relations between members
> of a family

III. USE THE WORD

1. The document was an obvious _____ and fooled no one.
2. Since the girl was under the legal age of consent, her assailant was automatically guilty of _____.
3. Having an affair with another man's wife is not only unethical, immoral, and dangerous; but also, since it constitutes the crime of _____, it is illegal.
4. When an unaccountable shortage was discovered in the company's funds, the treasurer was accused of _____.
5. George was greatly disturbed to realize his _____ desires toward his sister Ethel.

IV. WRITE THE WORD

1. Illicit intimate relations between mother and son   1. _____
2. Appropriation of funds entrusted to one's care by another   2. _____
3. Altering of the writing on a document for purposes of fraud   3. _____
4. Carnal knowledge of a woman against her will   4. _____
5. Carnal relations between two people, one of whom is married to another   5. _____

Check Your Learning

ANSWERS TO TESTS ON UNIT 23

TEST I
  1—false, 2—true, 3—true, 4—true, 5—false.

TEST II
  1—d, 2—b, 3—e, 4—c, 5—a.

TEST III
  1—forgery, 2—rape, 3—adultery, 4—embezzlement, 5—incestuous.

TEST IV
  1—incest, 2—embezzlement, 3—forgery, 4—rape, 5—adultery.

Unit Twenty-Four

MISCELLANEOUS LEGAL TERMS

121. **Plagiarism** (PLAY'-jee-ə-riz-əm): passing off as one's own original work, the literary composition of another. If a would-be writer copies a story from an old issue of a magazine, affixes his own name to it as author, and submits it for publication, he is a *plagiarist* (PLAY'-JEE-ə-rist). (This is not a far-fetched idea. It has happened on occasion that editors have received such *plagiarized* (PLAY'-jee-ə-rīzd) manuscripts in the mail, actually copied word for word from a very old issue of their own publication, have accepted and paid for it forthwith, and have published it, soon to receive hundreds of embarrassing letters from readers with longer memories than the editors'.)

It is considered *plagiarizing* (PLAY'-jee-ə-rīz-ing) also to copy, without due credit, any passages, substantial stretches of language, sequence of events in the plot of a story or novel, original diagrams or lists, etc.

(From Latin *plagiarius*, a kidnaper.)

122. **Mayhem** (MAY'-hem or MAY'-əm): legal term for the crime of maiming a person by depriving him of the use of any of his limbs or members, or of wilfully disfiguring any part of his body. For example, a woman who throws acid in the face of her rival for a man's affections is guilty of *mayhem*. (From an Old French word of similar meaning.)

123. **Larceny** (LAHR'-sə-nee): the general term for theft of any personal property, whether by burglary, robbery, embezzlement, swindling, etc. *Larcenous* (LAHR'-sə-nəs) acts are acts of thievery. In most states, a distinction is made between *grand larceny*, when the value of the property is over a certain amount (usually between $50 and $250) and *petty larceny*, when the property is of lesser value, with, of course, a proportionate difference in penalties. (From Latin *latro*, thief.)

124. **Libel** (LĪ-bəl): any untrue statement calculated to defame someone's character, or expose him to public ridicule, contempt,

hatred, etc. A distinction is often made between *libel* and *slander:* a *libelous* (LĪ-bə-ləs) statement or accusation, etc., is written, while a slanderous one is spoken. (From Latin *liber,* book.)

125. **Assault** (ə-SAWLT): unlawful threat or attempt to do bodily injury to a person, as by raising the arm or brandishing a club. It is merely *assault* if the actual injury is not carried out—once the hurt itself is inflicted it is called *battery.* (From Latin *salire,* to jump, plus *ad,* toward. This is the same root from which we derive *insult,* literally jump on, *desultory,* literally jumping around, and *exult,* literally jump out.)

126. **Seduction** (sə-DUK'-shən): the act of enticing another, by wiles, persuasion, or guile, to have unlawful sexual relations against his or her earlier opposition. This differs from *rape* in that no force or violence is employed. (From Latin *seduco,* lead away.)

127. **Blackmail**: extortion of money, by unlawful threats to expose someone's folly, weakness, crimes, etc., unless payment for silence is made. Despite the syllable *-mail* in this word, such extortion need not be made through the mails, the second syllable of the term having the old meaning, *payment.* From *black* plus *mail,* payment.)

128. **Commutation** (of sentence): the substitution of a lesser punishment for a more serious one, as life imprisonment for electrocution. Generally granted by the governor of a state or by the President. (Latin *muto,* to change.)

129. **Pardon**: an act by the executive power, as the governor of a state or the President, which releases a convicted offender from all punishment and disabilities prescribed by the court.

130. **Parole** (pə-RŌL'): the act of releasing a convict from prison before the termination of his punishment. The *parolee* (pə-RŌ'-lee), as the released convict is then called, is still subject to supervision by the public authorities for the remainder of his legal term, and may be returned to prison to complete his punishment if he violates any of the conditions of his *parole.* Such violation may be consorting with known criminals, becoming intoxicated, not reporting to his supervisor, engaging in crime, frequenting gambling places or race tracks, etc. (From French *parole,* word of honor, which the released convict gives that he will behave himself.)

Test Your Learning

From column II choose the term that applies to each of the acts in column I.

I	II

1. A man has been sentenced to the electric chair, but the governor of the state decrees that he may serve a certain period in prison instead.

2. A man, by offers of money, fancy clothes, etc., induces a woman to have unlawful relations with him.

3. An author models the plot of his novel directly on the plot of *Gone with the Wind*.

4. Someone cuts off the legs of a person he has kidnaped in order to prevent his escape.

5. John Doe knows that Richard Roe has a criminal record and threatens to expose him to his employer unless Roe pays him $200.

6. An editor recklessly publishes a vicious and false attack upon a motion picture actor, accusing him of indecent acts, lascivious behavior, adultery, rape, and seduction.

7. A woman goes into a department store and walks off with a fur coat worth $800—without paying for it.

8. During a heated argument, a man picks up a rock from the roadway and threatens to hurl it at his opponent.

9. A man has been convicted of forgery and sentenced to ten years in prison. At the end of five years of his term, he is released on condition that he submit to supervision of the proper public authorities for the next five years.

10. A man has been convicted of manslaughter and sentenced to life imprisonment. As there is considerable doubt that the convict is guilty

a—mayhem
b—libel
c—pardon
d—assault
e—plagiarism
f—parole
g—larceny
h—commutation
i—blackmail
j—seduction

of the crime for which he is being punished, the governor of the state orders his punishment revoked, the convicted criminal released, and all his civil rights restored to him.

Check Your Learning

1—h, 2—j, 3—c, 4—a, 5—i, 6—b, 7—g, 8—d, 9—f, 10—c.

Review Test VI

(A Complete Check on Your Understanding of Words 106–130)
Recall the words for which the definition and initial letter are given.

1. Appropriation to one's own use of money entrusted to one's care   E_____
2. Thievery of any sort   L_____
3. Illegal killing of a person, but without malice aforethought   M_____
4. The offense of a married person having an affair with a person other than his (or her) legal spouse   A_____
5. False statements under legal oath   P_____
6. Unlawful sexual relations between members of the same family   I_____
7. Theft from a person, in his presence, of property in his possession, by means of violence, threats, etc.   R_____
8. The offense of a man who forcibly and by violence consummates sexual relations with a woman   R_____
9. Malicious or fraudulent burning of one's own or another's building, home, etc.   A_____
10. A minor violation of law   M_____
11. A serious violation of law   F_____
12. Forcible or illegal entering of a premises for purpose of theft or other crime   B_____
13. Any killing of a human being   H_____
14. Fraudulent alteration of a document or copying of a signature   F_____

15. Unlawful contracting of another marriage while a previous marriage is still legally undissolved — B_____

16. Release of a convict before the termination of his prison sentence — P_____

17. Killing of a person with premeditation and malice aforethought — M_____

18. Passing off as one's own original work the literary property of another — P_____

19. Full release from punishment and other disabilities of someone convicted of a crime — P_____

20. Extortion of money through threats of exposure — B_____

21. Accusations in writing which tend to hold someone up to infamy, contempt, ridicule, etc. — L_____

22. Substitution of a lesser punishment for a greater one — C_____

23. Illegal disfiguring of the body of another — M_____

24. Threats or attempts to do bodily injury — A_____

25. Enticing of a woman into illicit relations — S_____

Check Your Learning

ANSWERS TO REVIEW TEST VI

1—embezzlement, 2—larceny, 3—manslaughter, 4—adultery, 5—perjury, 6—incest, 7—robbery, 8—rape, 9—arson, 10—misdemeanor, 11—felony, 12—burglary, 13—homicide, 14—forgery, 15—bigamy, 16—parole, 17—murder, 18—plagiarism, 19—pardon, 20—blackmail, 21—libel, 22—commutation, 23—mayhem, 24—assault, 25—seduction.

Final Examination
A Thorough Check of
Your Total Learning

Directions: In all sections, match the words in Column I with their meanings in Column II.

I	II
1. celibacy	a—immaturity
2. diffidence	b—confirmation
3. verbosity	c—sexual longing
4. puerility	d—disbelief in God
5. indolence	e—timidity owing to lack of confidence
6. corroboration	f—inordinate desire for wealth
7. renascence	g—truthfulness
8. cupidity	h—science of coins and medals
9. concupiscence	i—wordiness
10. atheism	j—laziness
11. numismatics	k—rebirth
12. veracity	l—avoidance of romantic encounters with the opposite sex

ANSWERS

1—1, 2—e, 3—i, 4—a, 5—j, 6—b, 7—k, 8—f, 9—c, 10—d, 11—h, 12—g.

SECTION 2

I	II
1. licentious	a—aimless
2. prodigal	b—insecure
3. desultory	c—out of existence or use
4. dilatory	d—unmanageable
5. obsolete	e—stubbornly uncompromising

6. precarious	f—unrestrained
7. frugal	g—pointless
8. recalcitrant	h—inborn
9. dogmatic	i—slow, delaying
10. inane	j—arrogantly positive
11. intransigent	k—wasteful
12. innate	l—economical

ANSWERS

1—f, 2—k, 3—a, 4—i, 5—c, 6—b, 7—l, 8—d, 9—j, 10—g, 11—e, 12—h.

SECTION 3

I	II
1. amplify	a—delay, postpone
2. debilitate	b—swear falsely
3. procrastinate	c—speak with excessive dignity
4. obliterate	d—steal funds in one's care
5. pontificate	e—turn to bone
6. ossify	f—pass off another's literary work as one's own
7. perjure	own
8. embezzle	g—weaken
9. plagiarize	h—reduce punishment
10. commute	i—wipe out completely
11. impede	j—get in the way
12. expedite	k—enlarge
	l—hasten

ANSWERS

1—k, 2—g, 3—a, 4—i, 5—c, 6—e, 7—b, 8—d, 9—f, 10—h, 11—j, 12—1.

SECTION 4

I	II
1. arson	a—serious crime
2. felony	b—release from punishment
3. misdemeanor	c—setting fire illegally to property
4. bigamy	d—sexual relations by force
5. homicide	e—sexual relations between members of a
6. burglary	family
7. robbery	f—thievery by illegal entry

185

8. rape	g—illegal disfiguring
9. incest	h—release from prison before end of sen-
10. mayhem	tence
11. pardon	i—minor infraction of law
12. parole	j—thievery from the person
	k—killing of a person
	l—illegal second marriage

ANSWERS

1—c, 2—a, 3—i, 4—l, 5—k, 6—f, 7—j, 8—d, 9—e, 10—g, 11—b, 12—h.

SECTION 5

I	II
1. seducer	a—hunter
2. iconoclast	b—one who enjoys inflicting pain
3. recluse	c—dancer
4. agnostic	d—one who dedicates himself to pursuit of
5. nimrod	pleasure
6. sadist	e—actor
7. voluptuary	f—fraud
8. masochist	g—girl swimmer
9. thespian	h—one who entices a woman into sexual
10. charlatan	relations by wiles or guile
11. terpsichorian	i—one who abnormally enjoys his own
12. naiad	pain or discomfort
	j—hermit
	k—mocker of tradition
	l—one who neither affirms nor denies a
	supreme being

ANSWERS

1—h, 2—k, 3—j, 4—l, 5—a, 6—b, 7—d, 8—i, 9—e, 10—f, 11—c, 12—g.

SECTION 6

I	II
1. nullify	a—make seem larger than in actuality
2. petrify	b—appease
3. vilify	c—charm
4. magnify	d—rot

186

5. deify   e—make void
6. putrefy   f—make happen suddenly
7. mollify   g—thunder against
8. captivate   h—make young again
9. precipitate   i—turn to stone
10. fulminate   j—accuse of baseness
11. rejuvenate   k—worship like a god
12. facilitate   l—make easier

ANSWERS

1—e, 2—i, 3—j, 4—a, 5—k, 6—d, 7—b, 8—c, 9—f, 10—g, 11—h, 12—l.

SECTION 7

I	II
1. stupefaction	a—desire for retaliation
2. amelioration	b—foreboding
3. reiteration	c—patient courage
4. incapacity	d—propriety
5. decorum	e—penitence
6. docility	f—repetition
7. vindictiveness	g—attachment
8. acerbity	h—inability to function
9. contrition	i—sharpness
10. premonition	j—manageability
11. adherence	k—amazement
12. fortitude	l—improvement

ANSWERS

1—k, 2—l, 3—f, 4—h, 5—d, 6—j, 7—a, 8—i, 9—e, 10—b, 11—g, 12—c.

SECTION 8

I	II
1. phlegmatic	a—untruthful
2. dour	b—rambling
3. contentious	c—unrestrained; cruel without provocation
4. prenatal	d—prior to birth
5. pedestrian (adj.)	e—uninspired
6. incoherent	f—emotionally dull
7. perfunctory	g—illegal and improper

8. mendacious	h—surprisingly great
9. prodigious	i—argumentative
10. illicit	j—false, though claimed genuine
11. wanton	k—severe, humorless, forbidding
12. spurious	l—unimaginative, slow, plodding

SECTION 9

I	II
1. admonition	a—morbid dread of confinement
2. preclusion	b—strong point
3. sanctimony	c—suspicion of all human motives
4. claustrophobia	d—a preventing of an occurrence
5. agoraphobia	e—science of stamp collecting
6. acrophobia	f—ballet arranging
7. forte	g—rebuke without hostility
8. cynicism	h—illegal killing with malice aforethought
9. philately	i—hypocritical virtue or piety
10. choreography	j—morbid dread of space
11. murder	k—illegal killing without premeditation
12. manslaughter	l—morbid dread of heights

SECTION 10

I	II
1. connoisseur	a—collector of relics of the past
2. Lothario	b—depth and richness of sound
3. bibliophile	c—cooperation
4. balletomane	d—promise of later success
5. antiquarian	e—judge of excellence
6. coquette	f—sexual relations between two people of whom one is married to a third person
7. sacrilege	
8. resonance	g—incompatibility
9. dissonance	h—ballet enthusiast
10. unison	i—seducer

11. auspiciousness	j—insincere flirt
12. adultery	k—violation of sanctity
	l—collector of books

ANSWERS

1—e, 2—i, 3—l, 4—h, 5—a, 6—j, 7—k, 8—b, 9—g, 10—c, 11—d, 12—f.

SECTION 11

I	II
1. castigate	a—extortion of money on threat of exposure
2. invalidate	
3. inherent	b—humorous in circumstances in which seriousness is expected
4. facetious	
5. incongruous	c—essential, inseparable
6. forgery	d—rebuke violently
7. larceny	e—untrue and base accusations in writing
8. libel	f—threats, by overt actions, to do bodily harm
9. assault	
10. blackmail	g—copying of another's signature for purposes of fraud
	h—thievery
	i—render null and void
	j—out of keeping with its surroundings

ANSWERS

1—d, 2—i, 3—c, 4—b, 5—j, 6—g, 7—h, 8—e, 9—f, 10—a.

Scoring

Allow one point for each correct choice on the 11 sections of the Final Examination. Maximum score is 130. Compute your learning success from the following chart.

115–130	Superior
95–114	Excellent
80–94	Good
65–79	Average
45–64	Below Average
0–44	Poor

Index